A manual of brain training, through scientific learning techniques, to enhance your Memory Power in three weeks. It is a catalogue of the innovative mind-boggling mechanisms and mnemonic methods by which one can improve one's memory power, improve concentration and revive creativity. A memorable book from a memory genius—it has the '*mantra*' to open up the secret layers of one's brain. A 'must' book for the young generation—especially students and the creative genre—aspiring to carve out an intellectual niche in this competitive world.

OUR BEST SELLERS

IMPOSSIBLE...POSSIBLE
Biswaroop Roy Chowdhury

This book is about change. People by nature are status quoists. It is a state of mind. But those who are able to change, they succeed faster than those who remain tied to their old habits, mindsets and prejudices. This book will tell you how you can change the way you think, act and behave. It requires a little effort. But the results will be phenomenal. The chronic patients can recover, the habitual failures can turn around and the die-hard pessimists can become incorrigible optimists.

VOCABULARY @ 100 Words/Hr
Biswaroop Roy Chowdhury

Whether you are a businessman, or a student, if you want to remember everything this book is a must for you. It deals with:
1. How to improve concentration
2. Memorizing difficult biological diagrams
3. How to study smarter not harder
4. Remembering long answers of history and geography
5. Preparing for competitive exams

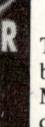

7 DAYS TO POWER MEMORY (with Audio Cassette)
Biswaroop Roy Chowdhury

This book helps you to increase your capacity to memorise in a better and efficient manner. The book teaches 100 Memory codes of Memory language which help the reader in developing a mental catalogue so that they can make their recalling and remembering efficient and effective. For students, businessmen and professionals this is a unique package. Just relax and listen to the cassette before reading and refer to this book whenever instructed by the cassette. Once you are through with the POWER MEMORY you will be on the road to better memory. Remember that!

MEMORISING DICTIONARY Made easy
Biswaroop Roy Chowdhury

"Memorising Dictionary Made Easy" will be immensely useful to all those who aspire to learn English & make their vocabulary comprehensive. The book identifies every new word with a 'Key' and a 'Memory Link', which connect the new word with a more identifiable word & in the process get firmly lodged in the reader's mind.

For Trade Enquiries & Catalouge contact
Publisher and Exporters of Indian Books, published more than 1000 titles.

⦿ FUSION BOOKS

X-30, Okhla Industrial Area, Phase-II, New Delhi-110020, Phone : 011-51611861, Fax : 011-51611866
E-mail : manish@diamondpublication.com, Website : www.diamondpublication.com

DYNAMIC MEMORY METHODS

Scientific Learning Techniques

Biswaroop Roy Chowdhury
National Memory Record Holder
(Limca Book of Records)

FUSION BOOKS

No part of this book may be reproduced or transmitted in any form or by any means electronic or mechanical including photocopying or recording or by any information storage and retrieval systems without permission in writing from **Fusion Books.**

ISBN : 81-7182-159-6

© Publisher

Published by : **Fusion Books**
X-30, Okhla Industrial Area, Phase-II
New Delhi-110020
Phone : 011-51611861-865
Fax : 011-51611866
E-mail : sales@diamondpublication.com
Website : www.diamondpublication.com

Edition

Price : Rs 175.00

Printed at : Adarsh Printers,
Navin Shahdara, Delhi-110032

Dynamic Memory methods   Rs. 150/
By Biswaroop Roy Chowdhury

Contents

Media Comments on Author's Work		9
1.	Introduction	13
2.	Memory and Brain	16
3.	How to Use This Book	18
4.	Age	19
5.	Mechanics of Remembering	22
6.	The Ten Principles for Better Memory	27
7.	The 'I' Factor for Strong Concentration	31
8.	Studying Smarter—The Brain's Way	33
9.	Revision— The Necessary Evil	34
10.	Break for Speed	36
11.	Suggesting Oneself to Success	37
12.	Memory Mechanism	38
13.	Imagination—A Perfect Retention Method	40
14.	Acronym—The Shortest Way to Learn	41
15.	The Reintegrating Process for Perfect Recall	43
16.	The Overlearning Principle	45
17.	Spider Notes	46
18.	Value of Incomplete Task	48
19.	Success through Latent Learning	49
20.	Developing the Power of Observation	50
21.	Concentration Exercise	51
22.	Mental Exercises to Develop Retention Power	52
23.	Using All the Senses	53
24.	Feeling Good	54
25.	The Creative Side	55
26.	How to Remember That Name	57
27.	The Sleep Trick That Works	58
28.	The Motor Mind	59

29.	Where Did I Keep My Keys?	60
30.	Break the Information Into Several Bits	62
31.	Memory Refresher	63
32.	Must Break the Night's Fast—Have Breakfast	64
33.	Memory Fruit	65
34.	Figurative Thinking	66
35.	Self Talk	67
36.	Potential Study Time	68
37.	Creative Debating Game	69
38.	Memory Signals	70
39.	Caffeine—The Memory Blaster	71
40.	Munch between the Meals	72
41.	The Deep Breath Method	73
42.	How to Develop Mental Storage Places for Things	74
43.	Delivering Speech without Notes	77
44.	The Weaker Side	79
45.	Charge Your Brain by Visiting a New Spot	80
46.	Go out of Routine	81
47.	Memory Power of Smell	82
48.	Memory for Numbers	83
49.	Effective Sleep for Effective Study	84
50.	Your Imagination Can Make It Happen	87
51.	The 2-Minute Stress Buster Chart	89
52.	Placebo—The Dummy Pill	91
53.	The Final Checklist for Exams	93
54.	The π Method	95
55.	Link Method for Formulae	96
56.	Clue Method—For Learning Foreign Languages	98
57.	Clue Method—For Vocabulary	101
58.	Memory Method for General Knowledge and Biological Terms/Definitions	102
59.	Learning Long Theories—The Keyword Method	104
60.	Remembering Scientific Data	106
61.	Memory Puzzle	109
62.	Marker Landmark Events	110

63.	Learn the Mnemonic Way	111
64.	Smart Memory for Spellings—I	112
65.	Memory Aid to Improve Spellings—II	115
66.	The Number Rhyme Method	117
67.	How to Use Rhyme Method	119
68.	The Number Shape Method	123
69.	The Value Method (41-60)	127
70.	The Alphabet Method (61-80)	129
71.	The Memorable Event Method (81-100)	131
72.	The Phonetics Method	134
73.	The Personalized Meaning System	137
74.	Indian Nobel Laureates	142
75.	How to Memorize Long Theory Having Data and Typical Names	144
76.	Mathematical and Scientific Data	147
77.	Generally Knowledge Often Confuses Us	159
78.	Remember Every Appointment	170
79.	Total Recall	174
80.	Common Memory Failures and Their Solutions	176

Media Comments on Author's Work

विद्या वही है जो कंठस्थ हो।

In fact education system has created pressure on students in which Memory can provide some rescue.

Dr. A.K. Sharma
Former Director NCERT

The greatest mystery of life is our ignorance of human brain. In fact brain is not a dustbin, but a gateway of some higher attainment.

This demonstration today by Biswaroop is an assurance that not everything is lost in the civilization.

Justice M.N. Venkatachelliah

The memory development techniques based on mnemonics customized by Biswaroop needs to be nurtured. With right platforms like Lion's Club etc., the techniques can be popularized in an amazing way globally for the benefit of mankind.

R.N. Lakhotia
Eminent Tax Expert

The principle in the book serves the purpose of education i.e. *Mukti* (मुक्ति), since the techniques mentioned in the book render the student more free time, as memorization becomes faster; hence the book should be included in NCERT curriculums and our basic education system.

R.K. Srivastava
Director Excel Hub.

Today in the arena of cut-throat competition memory development techniques customised by Biswaroop, a pioneer in the field of memory development, can surely rescue the overburdened students.

All India Radio—MW Yuv Vani (4th Aug. 1999)

इस नौजवान के पास है याददाश्त तेज करने का मंत्र

स्मृति हर किसी के पास है, दिक्कत सिर्फ यह है कि हम इसका प्रयोग कैपेसिटी यानि सामर्थ्य के मुताबिक नहीं करते।

सांध्य टाइम्स (22 जुलाई 1999)

स्मरण शक्ति बनाये रखने का गुर

पुस्तक में 100 ऐसे गुर हैं, जिनसे स्मरण शक्ति को हमेशा तरोताजा रखा जा सकता है। छात्रों के लिये यह बहुत उपयोगी पुस्तक है जो बताती है कि स्मरण शक्ति बनाये रखने के लिए वैज्ञानिक स्मरण शक्ति तकनीक का उपयोग कैसे किया जा सकता है।

राष्ट्र टाइम्स (25 से 31 जुलाई 1999)

डायनेमिक मेमोरी मेथड्स का विमोचन

सघन वर्षा और खराब मौसम भी जागरूक दिल्लीवासियों को रोक न सका और विश्व मेमोरी रिकार्ड प्रदर्शन की लालसा और मोह लोगों को पी. एच. डी. के प्रांगण में खींच लाया।

पंजाब केसरी (24 जुलाई 1999)

अगर आपको बार-बार भूलने की आदत सता रही है तो मिलें बिस्वरूप से जिनकी नई थ्योरी के मुताबिक किसी भी चीज को 3 भाग में 1 सेकण्ड में याद किया जा सकता है।

आंखो देखी (26 जुलाई 1999, DD-I)

"He has got the MANTRA to develop brain."
Dainik Tribune, October 2, 1997

"Biswaroop is a memory genius with a penchant for breaking records."
Indian Express, May 18, 1997

"Once you are through with Dynamic Memory Methods, you might well be on the road to a better memory."
Life Positive, August 1999

"Biswaroop, the memory master, demonstrated his findings on memory principles by helping audience learn complex sequences easily."
The Asian Age, January 9, 2001

"Biswaroop knows how to make the grey cells work."
The Times of India, January 7, 2001

"Combining the ancient wisdom and latest findings, Biswaroop has developed five techniques & memory language (shape learning), phonetic method (sound learning), personal meaning system (linking method), radiant thinking and advanced mnemonics system."
The Telegraph, January 10, 2001

"Biswaroop Roy Chowdhury, the man behind the books like Dynamic Memory Methods, is indeed a genius."
The Hindustan Times, February 18, 2001

"Biswaroop has memorized 600 years of the calendar."
India Today, January 22, 2001

1

Introduction

How to double your memory scientifically?

In today's arena of cut-throat competition, students spend most part of the day in studies, in spite of which they do not get desired results. Why?
- Failure to remember information
- Incorrect recall
- Inability to concentrate
- Ever-increasing syllabi.

Research: Capacity of Brain

According to one experiment, our brain can store upto two quintillion bits of information. That is two followed by eighteen zeros. It is equivalent to mastering forty languages, memorizing a complete set of encyclopaedia and complete graduation from dozens of universities. "The problem with us is not the capacity of the brain but our inability to manage that limitless capacity."

Solution

Scientists say we can compare our brain with a disorganized library which has all kinds of collection of books but with no catalogue or systematic arrangement, making the search for a particular book very difficult and sometimes impossible. The need of the hour is to build up a **Mental Catalogue** for our brain which can help us in learning everything very fast, improving our power of retention and helping in fast and correct recollection.

Some Evidences
- Dominic O' Brien, world memory record holder (*Guiness Book of World records*) holds innumerable world records in memory, including memorizing a pack of shuffled

playing cards in 40 seconds and memorizing 2000 binary digits in less than 30 minutes.
- A Russian journalist, Soloman Sherisheviskii, in the early nineteenth century, could tell at the age of 50, what he had been doing on every day of his last 25 years. He could even give exact dates and weather conditions during the day and say what he had eaten for breakfast, lunch and supper on any given day.

Were They Born with a Computer Memory?

Research and analysis has shown that people like Soloman Sherisheviskii and Dominic O' Brien were born with a very normal memory like anyone else but as children, they discovered the **Synesthetic Power**, through which they were able to learn everything fast, remember everything for very long periods and recall a particular information instantly even after 15-20 years.

What Is Synesthetic Power?

Answer: It is the in-built ability of our brain to receive particular information simultaneously through all the senses of our body and store it in a systematic manner by forming a kind of mental catalogue so as to make the remembering process 100 times more efficient.

Can We Develop Synesthetic Power?

Answer: In fact, we all are born with this power but only a few realize it and fewer were able to use it. What we need to do is direct this power in the formation of a mental cataloging system which can help us in our academic learning.

How to Achieve Super Power Memory for Exams?

A uniquely designed scientific step-by-step approach, the book, Dynamic Memory Methods, can help you in achieving a really powerful memory within three weeks.

The book teaches the reader how to use scientific memory techniques for memorizing faster and retaining it longer based on Mnemonics (artificial aids to learning) and laws of controlled association. The simple mental exercises mentioned in the book enhance the reader's observation and concentration in an amazing way. The regular practice of various techniques mentioned inculcates the habit of using the creative (Right) part of brain and thus the brain's capacity is optimized owing to the balanced use of both logical (Left) and creative parts of the brain.

Familiarity with memory tips can help readers remember telelphone numbers, vocabulary, names and faces, speeches and anecdotes or any other desired information.

Though useful for anyone interested in memory, some highlights include:
> *How to study smarter and not harder*
> *Advanced mnemonic system*
> *Preparing for competitive exams*
> *Creativity and you*
> *Remembering long answers of history, geograghical maps and biological diagrams*
> *Curing absent-mindedness*

Author's Appeal

I was born with a normal memory. At the age of 21, I got interested in memory techniques and started reading about the life history of great memorizers of the world like the Russian journalist, Soloman Sherisheviskii. Inspired by them, I tried to use the unique scientific memory techniques which they used in their life times. These techniques not only helped me in scoring outstanding marks in various exams and earning name, fame and money but also made me India's strongest memory man. Now I have put all those ancient scientific memory methods in my book **Dynamic Memory Methods**. It's your turn now to realize the true potential of your brain.

2

Memory and Brain

Just imagine what would happen if we suddenly lose our memory? Just stop and think about this for two minutes. During the second world war, many soldiers lost their memory through shell shock. People, who were on the point of drowning and were saved, relate that in a second their whole life flashed on their minds in vivid detail. This shows us how well the memory stores up impressions.

Our brain is like a huge library, containing lakhs of books. If you are to find a book of your choice from such a library, what could be the possible way? Yes, there is one and only one way to find a book from a library without a catalogue i.e., to go from book to book to see whether the particular book is there or not. In this process you may be able to find the book or you may fail to find it. In case you fail to find it, you will say that the particular book is not present in the library but the fact is you are just unable to locate the book, unable to trace the book. Similar is the case with our brain. Everything which we have seen, heard or felt is being secured permanently in one or the other part of the brain. But sometimes we are unable to recall or find the exact location of that data or thought and we say we have forgotten. For example, today you get introduced with someone, say, Mr. Gaurav, and after a lapse of time you again meet him in the market or in a park. It is quite possible that you are unable to recall his name and you simply say, sorry gentleman I know you somehow but have forgotten your name. At that instance, if that person gives you four options, that his name may be Ravi, Mohan, Gaurav or Krishan, you will instantly recall his name and say, 'yes you are Gaurav'.

This shows that you have not forgotten his name but the only problem was you were unable to trace his name in your memory. It happens, because we don't have any mental catalogue to refer to.

Whenever we have to recall something, we have to remember something, we just start searching it randomly in the library of our brain and the moment we are unable to find it, we assume that we have forgotten that particular thing.

So, friends, this means we need a mental catalogue for the ready reference, to make our recalling and remembering efficient and effective.

In the subsequent chapter, we shall learn how to make mental catalogue.

3

How to Use This Book

This book is an aid to learning. It will provide you with a memory tool, which can be used to memorize the things much faster and also retain it for longer.

The book is designed in a scientific way which involves the modern memory techniques to help you learn your syllabus. To get the maximum benefit from the book please follow the rules below:
1. Do not skip any chapter.
2. Each chapter should be read and a gap of one day should be taken between the reading of each chapter (during the gap day revise the previous chapter).
3. Gap between any two chapters should not exceed more than two days.
4. Do not skip any exercise.
5. Believe in the system.

4

Age

Must we accept a decrease in our efficiency, as we grow older? This question which confronts me a dozen times a day is usually asked by people who have passed their fiftieth birthday. Younger people are not much concerned about the future of their brain cells, and they cannot or will not realise that their own memory will not always remain so reliable as it is today.

Memorising is partly a physiological and partly a psychological process; and this dualism is responsible for the innumerable varieties of ways in which our memory works.

In the physiological sense memory rests on pathways connecting our brain cells, and both the quantity and the firmness of these pathways are decisive for its functioning. As we grow older, these brain-paths become less firm, and there comes a time when the process of forgetting proceeds more quickly than the process of learning.

While such an unwelcome reversal invariably happens near the end of a lifetime, there is much we can do to delay its occurrence. It is certainly not coincidence that many people who used their brains more than an average person, have kept their retentive and productive ability up to an extremely old age.

Think of Bernard Shaw, of Goethe, of Thomas Edison. It would be a fallacy to think that in order to take proper care of our brain cells we should spare them every effort and preserve them unused. Just the contrary holds true. You can train your brain as you train your muscles, and you can prove this to your satisfaction by simple tests while you go through the exercises described in this book. You will see that experiments which call for effort when tried for the first time become easy when you repeat them, and after a while you can hardly understand why they caused so much effort at all.

If we realise that memory can be developed like a muscle, we must also accept the truth that its efficiency will slacken like a muscle if it is not properly used. We all know that after an illness, which keeps us in bed for several weeks, walking is very difficult. The muscles of the legs forget how to move, and we have to relearn walking much as a little tot first masters the skill.

Why, then, should we be astonished when the same thing happens to our memory—when it loses its reliability if we don't use it? And yet the average adult is always afraid to trust his memory. There are notebooks and calendars, appointment books and telephone list, memorandum slips and desk notes—all destined to unburden our memory and therefore all working in the wrong direction.

Thorndike, who devoted much time to tests concerning memory and age, found that there is no natural reason for a decline, as we grow older except in the latest years of our lives. If our memory weakens before that time, we must blame ourselves. Let us admit that after we have left school we usually don't bother very much about learning anything—that is, learning in the actual sense of the word, not just reading, which is merely passive and receptive.

In practical adult life, except in acting and similar occupations, there is neither an inducement nor a motive for learning anything word to word. That in itself involves the loss of good memory techniques, which are connected only with steady practice. Still, this would not be decisive if we blanched it, at least, by remembering all the little things which occur in our daily business and social life. But, as I stated before, we are too much afraid to "burden our memory" and many of us consider it a waste of time to remember names and addresses, telephone numbers and appointments, which are so "much easier" jotted down and looked up in notebooks.

People take daily walks when it would be "much easier" to use the car or take a bus, because they know that walking is healthier and they wish to increase or at least keep up their muscular strength; on the other hand, they write down every little reminder, thus steadily decreasing their powers of memory.

If they try to remember something once in a long while, they are apt to forget it; as a consequence, they distrust their memory still more and they write down still more. In the end, they are astonished to find their memory failing them entirely, and they do not realise that they have only themselves to blame for this steady downward trend of memory and efficiency. All this, apart from physiological reasons, explains very well the fact that older people often forget important things which happened last month or even last week, while they remember perfectly every detail, even of unimportant events, which took place thirty or forty years ago.

5

Mechanics of Remembering

The object itself and the interest in the object are of greater importance for our memory, but equally important are the means of reception. We must distinguish among eye-minded, ear-minded and motor-minded persons and for any kind of learning and memorizing it is of utmost importance to know the types to which one belongs.

We call a person "eye-minded" if he remembers best the things which he sees, the stimuli, which are conveyed, to his brain cells by means of his eyes.

We call a person "ear-minded" if he remembers best the things which he hears, the stimuli, which are conveyed, to his brain cells by means of his ears.

We call a person "motor-minded" if he remembers best the things which are connected with a certain motion—either a motion which he carried out himself like writing or playing an instrument or a motion which is directed against the surface of his body, like the prick of a pin, or a sting of an insect.

It goes without saying that an eye-minded person profits most by learning from books, because his memory retains the printed words, sentences and paragraphs.

If he goes to a cinema, he will remember actions and incidents he saw on the screen, while the spoken word becomes hazy and fades away.

In contrast to him, the ear-minded person profits more by lectures than books, since his memory retains everything picked up through the ears. He may be able to repeat a conversation almost verbatim and at the same time have difficulty in describing what the person with whom he conducted this conversation looked like. If he attends a cinema, the sound of words and music will stay with him, while the actions are very soon forgotten.

Motor-mindedness refers to the remaining senses, which

are touch, smell and taste. With most of us they rank far behind sight and hearing, but of course there are exceptions. A blind person, being deprived of sight, usually develops all the other senses to a remarkable degree. This fact is important because it shows without the help of complicated tests that every sense can be developed and can be improved.

It must be understood that no human being is 100 per cent eye-minded, ear-minded, or motor-minded. We usually have all these qualities, and the only question is which of them is the preferment in a particular individual. We know that three quarters of all human beings are eye-minded but anywhere between 60 and 80%, while the balance is divided between hearing and remaining senses.

Among the people who are preponderantly ear-minded, musicians are foremost, especially those who are able to repeat a composition, which they have heard but whose score they have never seen.

It is interesting to note that the same types occur among animals. The eagle, for instance, relies for his survival entirely upon his marvellous eye, which enables him to detect his prey from an altitude so high that from where you or I could hardly distinguish a city from a forest. The deer's survival rests mainly on his ear, which catches the slightest shaking of a thing, whereas the dog has developed a sense of smell, which far surpasses his sight and hearing.

Although our way of learning and memorising any given material depends to a large extent on the type to which we belong, astonishingly, a few persons are really aware of their type. It is quite natural that a person who is preponderantly eye-minded should try to learn as much as possible from books and that a student who is preponderantly ear-minded makes better use of his time if he attends as many lectures as possible and listens to his professor's voice. However, as I said before, nobody is 100% eye, or ear-minded, therefore it is an advantage for the student who learns from books and reads aloud. If he does his ear will come to the aid of his eye, and he opens two channels to his brain instead of only one.

The motor-minded person will do best if he writes down as much possible. If he is eye-and motor-minded he may copy from his books, if he is ear-and motor-minded he should take notes while listening to the lectures. At any time, it is an advantage to know one's type and to arrange one's learning and memorising accordingly.

As I mentioned before, there are not too many persons who are aware of their types as far as reception is concerned. Ask a musician who plays a composition by heart how he does it, and in most cases he will answer that he does not know. However, if you insist that he examine what is going on in his mind while he is playing, you may hear all varieties of answers.

One pianist will tell that he sees or imagines the score before his mental eye while he is playing. He is the eye-minded type and he would be able to tell you without difficulty when the page should be turned. In contrast, the ear-minded musician follows his ear and it is quiet possible that he has never seen the score on that he would not be able to read it if he had, because he does not know musical notation. Finally, the motor-minded pianist would be able to play the composition even if the piano was mute. He relies neither on the score nor the melody. What he remembers best is the movement of his hands. The mechanical part of the pianist is at work.

I have often been asked how we can check our type if we don't know it. There are two procedures which I can recommend. One of them works better if you wish to test yourself, the other works better if you wish to test somebody else, for instance your friend etc.

If you wish to test yourself, select two paragraphs of equal length from a book; each of them may cover perhaps half a page. Read the first of these paragraphs silently to yourself. Check the exact time you need for reading it. Then write down on a piece of paper what you remember.

Having done this, ask somebody else to read the second paragraph to you while you listen. It is important to note that the time needed for the reading must be exactly the same as the time which you spent in reading the first paragraph. When your friend has finished his reading, write again on a piece of paper whatever you remember, then compare your two papers and see whether you remembered more of the paragraph you yourself read or the paragraph you listened to.

This experiment should be repeated at least three times. With each new experiment the material used should vary in length. If you used half a page the first time, choose a full page the second time and two pages the third time. It must be noted that the material used in one test reading and listening must always be of equal length.

The conclusion will be easy for you. If you find that you remember more of those paragraphs which you read for yourself, it means that you are preponderantly eye-minded; if you remember more of the paragraphs you listened to, it means that you are preponderantly ear-minded.

If you also wish to test whether you are motor-minded, copy the paragraphs in paper for an additional test.

It is somewhat easier to test someone else, especially if he does not know in advance what the test means. I am giving you a list of ten words, which you might read to him. Tell him only to write on a piece of paper the first word, preferably noun or verb, which comes to his mind when he hears a word that you call out to him. Here are the ten words: Wall, cake, book, noise, file, river, letter, bind, flag, and hat. Then look at the words, which your contestant wrote. Generally speaking, there are two possibilities:

A. He may have written words like these:
1. Picture, paper, ceiling
2. Flour, sugar, icing
3. Page, illustration, test
4. Propeller, music, serene
5. Paper, drawer, box
6. Water, boat, fishing
7. Envelope, typewriter, stamp
8. Feather, wings, egg
9. Cloth, mast, signal
10. Ribbon, straw, felt

B. He may have written words like these:
1. Hall, ball, value, valt
2. Make, bake
3. Look, hook, bug
4. Poise, choice, moist
5. Pile, mile, fine, fire
6. Liver, ringer
7. Latter, ladder, ledger, lecture
8. Flirt, hurt, birth
9. Bag, drag
10. Bat, chat, flat

Of course, all these words are only examples, and the variety of words which your contestant may have written in response to the words called out to him is almost unlimited.

But whatever his response is, a survey of his answer will show whether more words are similar to Group 1 or whether more words are similar to Group 2.

As you see, the examples which I gave in Group 1 contain

words which somebody with a vivid imagination may see if he thinks of wall, cake, book, and so on. The examples given in Group 2 indicate words which are similar in sound to the words which you called out to him. Therefore, if you check your contestant's papers, you must compare the words that you gave him with the words that he wrote down. If you find more words, which belong to Group 1, your contestant is preponderantly eye-minded. If you find more words which belong to Group 2, he is preponderantly ear-minded. By checking the number of words belonging in each of these two groups, you can even find the approximate percentage of his eye- or ear-mindedness.

You can also see why it is an advantage for your contestant not to know in advance the purpose of the test. If he knows it in advance, he will become too conscious of the association which he forms. He will watch to see whether he tends more to visual or to auditory associations, and such watchfulness is detrimental to the purpose of the test.

6

The Ten Principles for Better Memory

In order to remember well, in order to memorise effectively and efficiently, we must follow the following ten principles consciously:

I. Association

We know what a line is. If we put four lines of equal length together, end to end, we make a square. If we put six squares together, the result will be a cube. That is simple, isn't it? But nobody could understand the meaning of a cube without knowing what a line is and what a square is.

What is true in geometry is true in every phase of life. We learn and remember a thing that is new to us only by connecting it with something that we already know. There is no other way of acquiring knowledge.

You will immediately see the truth of this statement if you think of learning Sanskrit language. In order to learn that water is *Jal* in Sanskrit, we must form a connection between water and *Jal* and only if this connection or association is strong it will enable you to recall the Sanskrit word whenever we need it. Once the pathway between water and *Jal* is firmly established in our brain we will recall the one or the other without conscious effort, and even without our will.

Of course, I am fully aware of the fact that up to now you did not form such association consciously. Very frequently we are not even aware of forming associations at all. We do it subconsciously just as a little child connects the word **daddy** with his **father** without knowing anything about connection and associations.

However, we will see in the following chapters that it is to our advantage to form our association consciouly, and to form our connections in a way which fits our type and requirements of our own personal memory.

II. Confidence in Memory

Have faith in your memory, you must first have belief in your memory before you do something. Imbibe the following sentence firmly in your memory: **My brain is better than the best computer of this world.**

If you think you cannot remember something well, you will not remember well. You may have met people often over 45 years of age making a remark: "Excuse me, my memory is poor " or someone saying "I cannot recall your name" or "my memory is awful". The repetition of this statement that his memory is bad has adverse effect on his memory.

We should rather say to ourselves specially before and when we rise up in the morning: "I trust my memory as I know it can work as good as a computer".

One of the best ways to improve confidence in your memory is by means of auto-suggestion or repeating to yourself that "I remember better, I can remember better".

Just think how can we expect our memory to give service when we continually abuse it and tell everyone that my memory is bad. Having confidence in memory is so important that I wish to write the above statement twice but instead I am leaving a blank space for you to write...
....
....
....

III. Concentration

Concentration is nothing more than hard thought which is fixed upon one thing at a time. Erase everything else from your mind except that which you are seeing or hearing. Do not permit your thoughts to stray. Finally, see yourself physically depositing that memory in your mental memory bank and when you are able to do this, you are concentrating. We can compare concentration to making a donkey move. The more you push or pull, the more it resists. Similar is the case of our concentration i.e., the more we try to concentrate the more our thoughts stray, the trick of making a donkey move is to dangle a vegetable in front of him and he will follow wherever you feel like.

So, to concentrate on a particular subject we must create an interest in that subject.

IV. Power of Senses

You must clearly see and hear before you can make a memory deposit you will be able to withdraw later. Focus your sight on the object to be remembered and see it in your imagination, hear it, or perhaps taste or feel it. But in any case allow your senses to get into the act. When you permit your senses to become involved the impression is always keen and not easily forgotten. Try to involve all the following six senses while memorising or learning anything:

1. Sense of hearing
2. Sense of vision
3. Sense of smell
4. Sense of taste
5. Sense of touch
6. Sense of kinesthesia i.e., awareness of bodily position and movements.

V. Colour

We all dream and also we sometimes get involved in day-dreaming. Occupationally we try to analyze our dreams or discuss our dreams with friends. But have you ever given a thought regarding the colour of the dream whether the particular dream is coloured or just black and white.

Try analysing whether your dream is coloured or just black and white. If it is black and white try to see it again consciously in coloured then try to analyse whether a particular dream is very clear or faded. If faded, try to see it again in the screen of your imagination as clearly as possible. Whenever possible try to use full range of colours to make your picture and to make your thinking much more memorable.

VI. Exaggeration

It is the characteristic of our brain that it takes things in exaggerated form much more quickly and also retains that thing longer in our conscious mind.

So, why not use this characteristic in positive sense? Why not use this beauty of brain for remembering things better?

So, whenever possible, try to see the mental image in intensified form, in magnified form, in exaggerated form. Just imagine how difficult it would be to forget a fat person if we visualize his belly for a big pot and his face for a football.

VII. Picture

Try to form a mental image of whatever you want to remember. Form a mental image of the thought, date, theory or anything else you want to memorise because making of mental image makes the memorising process fast.

Whenever possible, try to visualize the things in motion.

VIII. Sex

Sex is a field of common interest. We all have good memory in this field. So, use sex as an aid to memory whenever possible.

IX. Oddities

Let's say you are a student and one day your teacher delivers the lecture with his helmet on his head. You will agree with me that you will never forget that day. This is an oddity.

It is the beauty of the brain that it accepts silly, odd things quickly and also retain it for longer duration, so why not use this characteristic for memorising things.

Nothing in life is so dull or serious that it can't be made into something that's fun to remember. When something is humorous, recollection becomes easy because it is fun.

X. Thoughts

If not altogether impossible you will agree with me that it is very difficult to memorize abstract thoughts. Therefore, it is vital to convert the abstract thoughts into some mental picture and then this mental picture will help us to recall the abstract idea we want to remember.

Basically, we cannot deposit anything in our memory until we reduce it to something we understand, then to something we can see or picturise. Trying to deposit a thought without understanding is trying to deposit foreign money in our own bank account. To deposit foreign money in our own bank account, first we have to exchange it and convert it into equivalent Indian currency.

Similarly, to deposit an abstract idea, first we have to convert it into something which we can understand, then to something we can visualize; only then our brain will accept it effectively.

7

The 'I' Factor for Strong Concentration

Do you have a strong concentration power? I asked this question to about 50,000 students in the last three years. As many as 99% of students answered—No!

Now Read This

When we go to see a movie of our choice, we are able to concentrate for 3 hours. We hardly know who is sitting beside us and when he has got up, etc. When we watch a cricket match, again we are thoroughly absorbed. At the same time, when we are studying, specifically a lengthy topic, we feel easily distracted even by music which is being played miles away in a very low volume.

All these experiences suggest that concentration is nothing but the amount of interest for the subject.

Amount of learning is dependent on amount of concentration and the amount of concentration is dependent on the amount of interest.

The equation is

Learning α Concentration α Interest

The next important question could be:

How to develop interest in a boring subject so as to develop concentration?

Understand this to understand interest:

Imagine that you are given photographs of last week's party of which you were also a part.

What will you look for in all the photographs?

Simple, you will look for yourself in the photographs.

Our interest is most of the time in 'I' or something associated with 'I'.

We can learn a subject quickly when we associate ourself with the subject.

How to Do That

In one of my memory tests, I taught two sets of Class VI students about "Early men and their evolution".

To Set I, I just narrated the story like this:

"Early men used to live in caves. They discovered fire by rubbing one stone against the other stone. They used to wear leaves and animal skins...."

I asked Set II to think of themselves as early men and narrated to them:

"You lived in caves. You discovered fire by rubbing one stone against the other stone. You wore leaves and animal skins".

The Result

On an average the Set II students learnt the lesson faster and were able to reproduce it almost correctly even after a year.

Keyword: Involve yourself.

8

Studying Smarter—The Brain's Way

Imagine you are going to appear for an exam after six days and you have five subjects (of equal length) to study. Which of these methods will you opt for?

Method I: Studying and completing one subject a day for five days and making a final revision on the sixth day of all the subjects.

Method II: Every day studying a combination of subjects—like two hours History, then next two hours Mathematics, etc.

Let us analyse and understand the brain.

The Analysis

When we study a particular subject, say Mathematics, a particular part of the brain is working more than the rest of the brain. When we shift to say History, practically the other part of brain would become active and the part studying Mathematics will go for rest.

By frequently changing the subject, we give a chance to refresh a particular part of the brain and also prevent ourselves from feeling tired.

Conclusion

If we study a particular subject throughout the day, we stress a particular part of the brain more which is inefficient and undesirable. So, study a combination of subjects, i.e., after studying Mathematics for 2-3 hours shift to Geography or Civics for two hours.

Keyword: Combination of subjects

9

Revision—The Necessary Evil

We must accept the fact:
"The strongest memory is not as good as the weakest link":
Unless we revise, it has no value.

Here comes the importance of revision. Although we all know the importance of revision but the important thing is revising scientifically for the best result.

The Scientific Revision Method

Let's try to understand it with an example.

Let's say, I take around two hours to learn a particular topic by heart. When should I revise it?

Scientifically speaking, the first revision should be done by the end of twenty-four hours.

On an average the brain is able to retain the newly learnt information up to the 80-100% only for twenty-four hours. The forgetting cycle becomes faster as soon as twenty-four hours end. So, the first revision must be at the end of twenty-four hours of the learning.

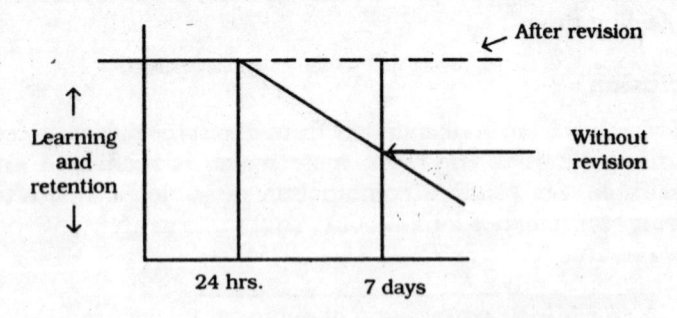

Further, once revised after twety-four hours, now the brain is able to hold it for approximately seven days, then the forgetting cycle once again becomes faster. So, the next revision must be after seven days.

Interestingly, if you revise at these two periods—i.e., the first revision after twenty-four hours and then the next after seven days—your revision time will be just 10% of the total learning time (in this case you will require just twelve minutes to revise the material).

Keyword: 24 hours/7 days

10

Break for Speed

A planned series of learning during a study period, increase the probability of recall. A break after every 40-50 minutes is optimum and each break could be of the order of about 10 minutes. Further, a break should be a complete rest from the type of study being undertaken, otherwise too many competing or interfering associations will be formed and they will confuse the memory track laid down in the study period. In the break, one may go for listening to music or having a little physical movement or breathing and relaxation exercise.

Why Break Works

Zeigarnik, a German researcher, found that interrupting a task in which a person was involved, even if that task is going well, can lead to appreciably higher subsequent recall.

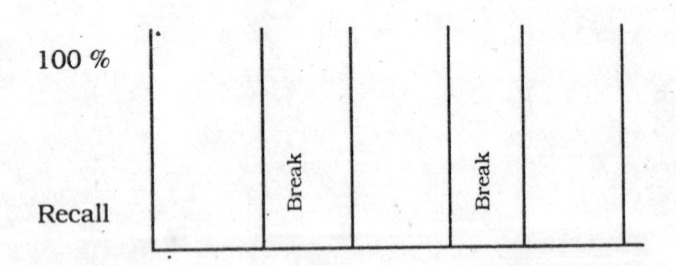

Break acts like a pillar which holds the information learnt.

Keyword: 45 minutes/10 minutes

11

Suggesting Oneself to Success

Frequently, I come across this question:
"How effective are the various memory enhancement medicines?" or "Do these memory tonics or tablets really help"?

To find out the effectiveness of those memory development medicines, I did an experiment.

I collected a group of 30 people—all of same age group and from similar backgrounds. I told them that I have a memory tonic which can improve their memory in three months. Then, I took small memory tests and gave fifteen of them a very popular brand of memory tonic and the remaining fifteen plain coloured water in the same branded bottle. All of them continued the given drink for three months. After that I took the similar memory test.

Result

Score of memory test of both the groups increased equally.

Conclusion

It was just a psychological factor. All of them believed that since they were doing something extra for their brain, they must get some extra result.

It is this belief, confidence and faith in oneself which help a person in performing better.

Also remember the words of Henry Ford:
"Whether you think you can or you think you can't you are right."

Keyword: Auto-suggestion

12

Memory Mechanism

What is memory? What results in the feeling of being learnt? How do we remember the things we remember? Did you ever question your memory about memory?

Answer

Memory is nothing but connection of new thoughts/ information with the thoughts/ information which are already stored in the brain.

Law of Association

We learn a new data only when it gets linked/associated with the data which is already stored in the brain. And that linkage or connection is called memory. For instance, you happen to visit your childhood school building. The very veiw of it will make you recall the associated experiences. The key to the recall is the connection of your experience with the school building.

The Chain Method

Let's say you want to learn the following list of words in the same order.

1. Dog	2. Shoes	3. Movie
4. Dragon	5. Cycle	6. Telephone
7. Pen	8. Cold drink	9. Tiger
10. Tape recorder		

Method I

One way of learning this is by repeating it till it is learnt. It may take about 25 repetitions which may ensure a perfect recall even after 2-3 days.

Method II

The second way is to form an association between the words. For example:

Imagine a <u>DOG</u> wearing <u>SHOES</u> and going for a <u>MOVIE</u> of a <u>DRAGON</u>. In the movie, the <u>DRAGON</u> is riding a <u>CYCLE</u>. The cycle hits a <u>TELEPHONE BOOTH</u>. A person repairs the telephone with the tip of a <u>PEN</u>. Now think that the pen is filled with <u>COLD DRINK</u> and not ink. You are serving cold drink to a <u>TIGER</u>. The tiger is dancing to the tune of a <u>TAPE RECORDER</u>.

Do you need to read it again?

Isn't that simple? Surely, Method II is more efficient than Method I but one thing is common in both the methods, that is association. In the first method, the words got associated automatically/subconsciously with the other stored information of the brain. Hence, you may confuse the order later on. In Method II you made a deliberate attempt to learn the words with conscious association.

Conscious association is better than subconscious or no association.

Conclusion

Always try to connect the new information you want to learn with something (else).

| **Keyword:** | Conscious association |

13

Imagination—A Perfect Retention Method

Every invention is first invented in imagination than in reality. The imagination is literally the workshop wherein all plans created by man are fashioned. Man's only limitation, within reason, lies in his development and use of his imagination. Imagination is an intangible force, but it has more power than the physical brain that gives birth to it. It has the power to live on even after the brain that creates it has returned to dust. *Use this power in learning.*

Visualization

Whatever you read, try to convert that into a picture and visualize it. Our eye memory is stronger by 20 times than the ear memory since the nerves connecting brains to eye are stronger by 20 times than nerves connecting ears to brain. This method can be best used in subjects like History. For instance, if you need to learn all about the Harappan civilization, read, understand and construct the civilization mentally in your mind. Try to live in that.

Always ensure that whatever you read, you have something in picture to relate to. Hearing makes us learn the thing. Seeing and imaginig the same makes us remember the thing for long.

Visualization has helped me in making a national record in memory for perfect retention. So, always picture a thing in the mind.

Keyword: Visualization

14

Acronym—The Shortest Way to Learn

If you want to remember the seven most important rules of learning, here they are:
1. Concentration
2. Interference law
3. Spaced learning
4. Revision plan
5. Seeing/Visualization
6. Association
7. Sleep

To remember these rules, the best way is to form an acronym with the first letters of each word:

C- Concentration
I- Interference
R- Revision plan
C-
U-
S- Spaced learning
A- Association
S- Seeing
S- Sleep

By just committing CIRCUS ASS to your memory, you can remember all the seven rules of learning.

Don't worry about the unused letters like the second C or U (in this case).

While recalling automatically your brain will separate the unused letters.

Try to form your own word (acronym) for the next seven rules.

8. Overlearning
9. Reintegration
10. Incomplete learning
11. Mapping

12. Latent learning
13. Clue method
14. Concentration exercise

Keyword: First letter of word

15

The Reintegrating Process for Perfect Recall

"I go from one room to another to collect something but the moment I reach there, I am unable to recollect what I came there for. I go back to the same room from where I started, now once again it appears."

"I rush to the refrigerator or cupboard to take a particular thing but find myself unable to recollect the moment I open it. I close the refrigerator/cupboard, move back 3-4 steps, now it appears once again. I go and finally get the thing from it."

These are some of the statements which I usually hear from many people.

Why does it happen?
How to avoid it?

Analysis/Findings

Findings suggest that our brain is in a better position to recollect information when it (our brain) is in the same surroundings in which it has learnt it. So, when we go back to the initial location we instantly recall the matter. This particular phenomenon of the brain, of better recollection in similar or same surroundings in which it has learnt a particular data, is called reintegration.

Why are we sometimes unable to hold the information even for a few seconds before we arrive at the spot to collect it?

Answer

Our mind is a thinking machine. May be that, at that moment, you were busy thinking something else (absent-mindedness) which has interfered with the base information of collecting a particular thing.

How to Use Reintegration in Studies

Sometimes, in an examination hall, we are unable to recall a particular answer which we have learnt earlier. We struggle hard but all in vain. I suggest you to concentrate and mentally go back to the surroundings (your study table or library) in which you have originally learnt it. Then further mentally VISUALIZE yourself opening that page of the book and then try to read the page mentally.

It should not take more than 10 seconds to complete the imaginary reintegration process.

Keyword: Revisiting

16

The Overlearning Principle

You take up a new topic to learn. Spend 15 minutes repeating until you are able to recollect it correctly without looking at the matter. *What do you do then?* Shift to some other thing.

According to the law of overlearning, we should spend at least 1/3 time (1/3 of the original learning time) more repeating the same material immediately after the learning.

For instance, in this case, you are suggested to repeat it for 5 more minutes (5 minutes is 1/3 of 15 minutes). Material overlearnt this way can help you in saving a lot of revision time and also improve your retention for that particular matter.

And also specifically we find ourselves short of time in examinations not because of our inability to write fast but because of our inability to recall fast.

Overlearning also helps in fast recollection.

Keyword: 1/3 time more

17

Spider Notes

This is one of the most effective ways of note making. The final notes should always be in condensed form, at the same time they should include all the important information so as to help in subsequent and final revision before the exams.

In spider notes, the *primary idea* is placed in the centre of the page so that the *secondary* and *tertiary ideas* can follow quickly and easily facilitate a harmonious thought process. (See the spider notes of first few chapters in the next page.)

Advantages of Spider Notes over Linear Notes

1. About 65% time is saved by noting only the relevent words.
2. About 90% time is saved by reading only relevant words.
3. About 90% revision time is saved.
4. About 85% time is saved by not having to search for keywords amongst unnecessary verbiage.
5. Essential key words are more easily discernible.
6. Concentration on real issue is enhanced.
7. Quick and appropriate association is made between the keywords.
8. The brain finds it easier to accept and remember visually stimulating, multidimensional spiders, rather than monotonous, boring linear notes.

Keyword: Spider notes

Dynamic Memory

- **Revision** — 24 hrs/7 days
- **Spaced learning**
- **Spider notes**
  - Less time to make
  - Less space
- **Visualization**
  - Colour
  - Eye
  - Mental image
- **Reintegration**
  - Fast recollection
  - Going back mentally
- **Association**
  - Subconscious
  - Conscious
- **Acronym** — Circus Ass
- **Overlearning** — Spending 1/3 times more
- **Concentration** — Involvement
- **Interference** — Combination of subjects

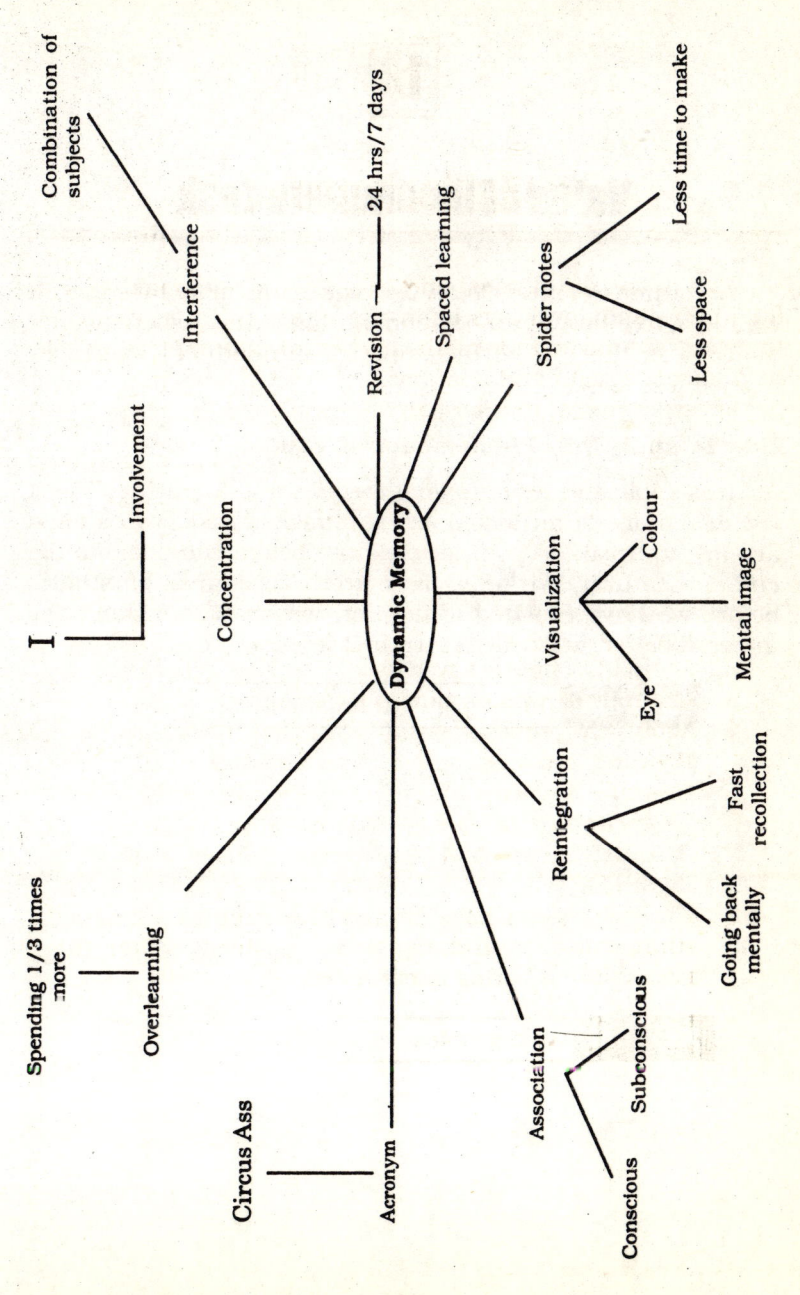

18

Value of Incomplete Task

According to Freud, "A failure makes one more inventive. It creates a free flow of associations, brings ideas, whereas once success is there a certain narrow-mindedness or thick-headedness sets in".

How to Apply This Phenomenon to Studies

It is applicable more to long theories and literature. To get the advantage of an incomplete/unfinished task, you should arrange to break off your studies just before you come to the end of a natural division of the matter. If we break off studies before we have finished a chapter, we shall remember the material better, when we return to it later.

Keyword: Incomplete/unfinished task

19

Success through Latent Learning

"Great athletes acknowledge that 60-90% of success in sports is due to mental factor". (*Psychologist Charles Garfield*) This is true not only in sports but in every field. A positive and definite day dreaming and self suggestion can lead us to our goals faster.

How to Use Latent Learning in Exams

The night before the exams, take five minutes for latent learning and complete the following steps:
1. Close your eyes and imagine yourself walking towards the examination centre, finding your seat and finally getting seated.
2. Visualize clearly the examiner approaching and handing you the Question/Answer sheet. Ensure you see everything in bright.
3. Now mentally open and read the instructions and the questions.
4. Put positive suggestions and imagine that you are correctly answering all the questions and finishing them in time.

This way of rehearsing in the mind the complete process actually helps in improving the performance and builds confidence.

(Also see relevant chapter: *Imagination—A perfect retention method*)

Keyword: Mental rehearsal

20

Developing the Power of Observation

"Sometimes, I am confused thinking whether it was the street no. 3 or 4. I am unable to recall the colour of a friend's shirt which he wore yesterday. Where did I place my watch? Which side is the physics book section in the library?"

Sometimes we are confused about these and other similar things.

Remedy

We need to develop strong observation skills.
The following mental activities can surely be a rescue:
1. Look at the shop window and try to estimate (without counting) the number of articles on display.
2. Estimate the weight of objects like glass, pen, books, eatables, etc.
3. Touch various articles with your eyes closed and try to identify the type of articles. Decide which kind of material they are made of. Try to identify the various qualities without the help of your eyes.
4. Train your ability to estimate the distance while you are taking a walk. Estimate how many steps it take you to reach a certain house, tree or lamp-post, etc. Count your steps and check that. If you are wrong try to do better next time.

Keyword: Estimation

21

Concentration Exercise

Concentration is like a donkey. The more you push or pull, the more it opposes. Similarly, the more you try to force your concentration on a particular subject, the more it will go away from it.

The best way to concentrate is not by using force but by generating interest in the subject (Also see the chapter: *"I" factor for strong concentration*).

Boost Your Concentration

Here I suggest a few concentration exercises which can boost your concentration:
1. *First week:* Place a clock on a television, playing the news or a serial, etc. Try to focus your attention on the movement of the seconds hand of the clock for 5 minutes. Don't allow the television to steer the focus of your attention. Try to do this exercise for a week.
2. *Second week*: Place half of your attention on the seconds hand of the clock and the other half on the number series 3,6,9... juggling both the things in the mind. If you lose track after a while, just restart the exercise. Do the exercise for 5 minutes. Every time you do the exercise, change the value of the series, e.g., 4, 8, 12, 16... or 3, 7, 11, 15... Do it for a week.
3. *Third week*: Concentrate on the motion of the seconds hand with one-third of your attention. With another one-third of the concentration, sing a song. With the remaining third of your attention, focus on a number series. Do it for a week.
4. *Fourth week*: Invent your own concentration exercise.

Keyword:	Clock exercise

22

Mental Exercises to Develop Retention Power

Students always complain that they are able to learn but unable to retain for a long time. They confuse more when the volume is huge. Also, whenever we come across a new telephone number we immediately go for penning it down as we are not confident of retaining the small eight-ten digits figure even temporarily.

For that matter the following exercises can be of use:

Mental Exercise I

Mentally recite (without using pencil or pen) the following number series:
Down by 2, up by 2: 100-2, 98-4, 96-6, ...2-100.
Every time you do the exercise, just change the initial values of the numbers, e.g., Down by 3, up by 2: 99-2, 96-4, ...3-66.

Mental Exercise II

Recite a triple ascending series:
Up by 2, 3, 4: 2-3-4, 4-6-8, 6-9-12, 8-12-16, ...48-72-96.

Mental Exercise III

Recite a triple alternating series:
Down by 2, up by 4, down 3: 100-4-99, 98-8-96 52-100-28.

Mental Exercise IV

Recite a quadruple series:
Up by 2, 3, 4, 5: 2-3-4-5, 4-6-8-10, 6-9, 12-15,.....40-60-80-100.

Keyword: Number series

23

Using All the Senses

According to Dr. Bruno Frost, on an average we remember:
- 25% of what we read.
- 35% of what we hear.
- 50% of what we see.
- 60% of what we say.
- 75% of what we do.
- 95% of what we read, hear, see, say and do.

So, try to use more of your senses.

Synesthesia

Russian journalist Mr Soloman Veniaminovich Shereshevskii (known as Mr S) is a perfect example of using all the senses. He had such a perfect memory that if he was asked what had happened on a particular day 15 years back, he would pause for a moment before asking back at what time. And given the time he would not only be able to narrate the whole incident perfectly but also he would be able to tell the colour of the dresses of the people who were present at that particular moment.

The secret was he had an incredible capacity for visualization and synesthesia. Synesthesia is the ability to express a memory generated in one sense in terms of another—sounds expressed as colours, for example.

Whenever, information was presented to Soloman, he encoded it in a very elaborate manner with rich associative images.

The result was vivid and highly interactive imagery. So, the more sensory channels you can learn in, the better you will learn. Start perhaps with the visual image, then link it with a sound, feeling and then if possible with taste and smell. The more the association, the more the mental hooks on which to hang your new knowledge, and the more retrieval clues you have for fast recall when you want it.

Keywords: See, smell, taste, feel

24

Feeling Good

Enjoyment makes life worth living. It helps us feel better about ourselves, and it enables us to learn more from our experiences. According to a study, people from various fields like artists, athletes, chessplayers, musicians, engineers and doctors were interviewed about how they feel when they are doing what they enjoy. Their descriptions of enjoyment were similar in spite of the fact that their activities were varied.

During the state of enjoyment you often cease to be aware of anything outside the activity in which you are engaged. Self-consciousness and self-doubt disappear and you are likely to lose all awareness of time.

It is important to create rewarding experiences for yourself, to have an enjoyable atmosphere in which to engage in mental activities.

Any mental activity that "feels good" to you is a reward and will induce positive changes in the brain, ranging from the release of natural opiates to the consumption of more brain enhancing oxygen and nutrients. The memory created by these neural changes make it easier for you to engage in the mental activity the next time you attempt it.

Keyword: Enjoyment

25

The Creative Side

Our brain is divided in two parts, i.e., the left side or the logical part and the right side or the creative part.

Step by step thinking
Calculation
Rote learning
Sequencing
Logics

(Logical)   (Creative)

Dreams
Fantasy
Imagination
Colours
Creation

As a student, teacher or a professional most of the time we are logical and accomplish all the activities using the left brain. Hardly is it that we are creative.

A constant ignorance of one part of the brain may lead to overall depletion of brain performance.

I suggest you to go for some creative activity every day for a healthy brain.

Exercise 1

For the next two minutes and as fast as you can, think of every single possible use of a paper-clip. Finish this exercise and check your result.

If your score is between

3 to 5	→	Average creativity level
7 to 8	→	Good brainstormer
12	→	Exceptional and rare
16	→	Thomas Edison level!

Open Your Mind

Look again at the question: "Think of every possible use you can for a paperclip". The more rigidly taught mind will assume that 'use' refers to the standard, ordinary, sensible applications for a paperclip. That same rigidly taught mind will also assume that the paper-clip is of a standard size and is made of standard material. A very standard, normal thinking, "What is the creative test trying to measure?" Thoughts that are removed from the norms. The creative, intelligent, and therefore more flexible-minded will see far more opportunities for creative interpretations of the question and so will generate both more ideas, and ideas which are of higher quality. The creative mind will expand the memory of the word 'use' to include the phrase connections with it.

Such a mind will also realise that a paperclip could be of any size and could be made up of any material and be transformed into any shape.

The creative mind will, therefore, break all the boundaries, and will include in the list of uses many 'far-out' applications—such as converting a very huge flexible paperclip into a rod chair.

Try to do the above exercise with a pen, glass or telephone booth, etc.

Exercise II

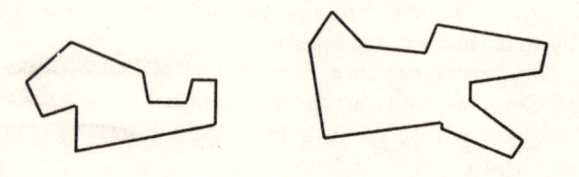

Concentrate on each of the randomly drawn figures and try to think of an object or a thing which it resembles.

Keyword: Break boundaries

26

How to Remember That Name

"Yah, I know that you are working with Telco, live in Preet Vihar and we met about 2 months back in India Habitat Centre, but sorry gentleman, I am unable to recollect your name."

Does it ever happen with you?

You are not always expected to recollect everybody's name the next time you meet him but nevertheless it would be advantageous to address a person with his name the next time you meet because the sweetest sound for a person is his own name.

How I Remember Names

The moment I am introduced to a person or hear some name, let me say, Sanjay, immediately I go for the following mental process:

Step I: I try to identify a person whom I already know by this name like in this case actor Sanjay Dutt or my friend Sanjay Paul.

Step II: I try to connect/associate the known person (Sanjay Dutt or Sanjay Paul in this case) with the new individual that I do just by visualizing the two standing or dancing together, etc. This whole process should not take more than 2-3 seconds. Now I will remember the name and the individual because by doing this I used the three fundamental principles of memory.

 a. Association
 b. Making the thing outstanding/silly
 c. Visualization.

Applying these principles,
 1. Get the name clearly.
 2. Repeat the name immediately after introduction.
 3. Repeat the name several times.
 4. See whether the name has a meaning in itself.
 5. Connect the name with the face.

Keyword:	Attention

27

The Sleep Trick That Works

Effective sleep is a must for effective studies. Often, students complain by saying that many times they face the problem—sleeplessness. *Is there a technique to fall asleep as soon as you go to bed?*

To find out the answer I studied numerous books on effective sleep and sleeping habits and also experimented with the suggestions I got. Following are the suggestions:

Suggestions

1. Do a little meditation just before sleep.
2. Read a boring book.
3. Visualize black colour (or no colour) in mind.
4. Drink milk just before sleep, etc.

All these suggestions did not work. Then I got the required key from one of the books on sleep. It says: "While in the bed close your eyes after switching off the lights and think that I will not sleep tonight". Yes, think again, "I will not sleep tonight", think of it continuously. It will not take more than 5 minutes before you fall asleep but don't count the time.

The principle which works here may be debatable but one thing is sure that you will definitely have a sound sleep. Many of my students find it beneficial.

So try it the night you are concerned by the problem of sleeplessness.

(Also read the chapter: *Effective sleep for effective studies*)

Keyword: Think opposite

28

The Motor Mind

You already know that exercises strengthen the muscle and cardiovascular tone, improve your body's abilities to use nutrients and oxygen and make you look great.

While we all know the physical effects of exercising our body few of us stop to consider what mediates those effects—the brain.

Brain Mediates Physical Effects of Exercise

When you exercise any mental function, the brain cells that control that function become active and develop cellular memories of the exercise.

If you are engaged in a physical activity, e.g., playing a piano or cycling or dancing or anything that requires coordinated movement, you have noticed that your performance gets better with practice. Your movement becomes quicker and less prone to error.

The basis of your performance was not in your muscles but in your brain. As relevant nerve cells developed their adaptive memories of your physical exercise, the movement they controlled became more fluent and decisive. Obviously, then, the more activities you are willing to try to learn, the more you will increase the neural adaptation of larger numbers of brain cells.

Physical exercise thus builds not only its own neural adaptation, enabling you to get better at the specific activity in which you are engaging, but it also stimulates the plasticity of brain cells in connected brain system that you can call on for a wide range of uses in the future.

Keyword: Physical exercise

29

Where Did I Keep My Keys?

"I am unable to locate my book which I kept somewhere only yesterday. I could not find the pencil or the spectacles."

Almost every day, we spend some part of our precious time in searching for our belongings. It is a very common memory problem and we would definitely like to get rid of it.

Why It Happens

This is called absent-mindedness, i.e., absent mind. Look at the problem from a logical angle.

While you were keeping your keys, possibly your mind was thinking of something else. At the very first place, the mind has not registered at all the placement of the keys. So why should you expect to recall something which you have never learnt?

The absent-mindedness problem is more likely to happen when you are overburdened with work or when you are trying to do too many things in very little time or when you are tense or worried about something. In all the above cases, the mind is preoccupied and hence is unable to register the body's physical movement (like moving of hand towards table to keep the keys, etc).

Solution

You can save yourself from absent-mindedness by following these steps:

Step I: Try to avoid all the above situations which may result in absent-mindedness and always be systematic and practical.

Step II: Stop worrying (Read chapter: *The 2-minute stress buster chart*).

Step III: At that moment, when you are unable to find a particular thing, stop panicking and instead, with open mind, visualize back (like reverse movie) in a step-by-step manner.

Imagine what you did just before and after placing that particular lost object.

This exercise will automatically bring you closer to the place where you have kept that particular thing.

Keyword: Present-mindedness

30

Break the Information into Several Bits

Our brain has a peculiar system to locate a particular information. Any information that is passed on to the brain by breaking it into various sensory stimuli—visual, auditory, etc.—is likely to be glued for a longer period and that too with its vivid details. It is so because each sense stimulus is stored in a specific part of the brain.

Allow your senses to interact with as many of senses as you can. Use your sense of sight, sound, smell, touch, taste (wherever possible) and also the body movements and positions. You can also make emotional connections. It is likely that Mr Rajan's face or name reminds you of your primary teacher. Using this method of association, one is more likely to remember things. You can also help plant the name in your brain by addressing him by name during your conversation. You can say, "Pleased to meet you, Mr Rajan".

Breaking the information into lots of bits and recalling it with a holistic approach will help tremendously.

Keyword: Bits

31

Memory Refresher

Do you know what are the two most important things for our lives? Yes, they are air and water.

Regarding water, it is present in all parts of our body but is found in larger quantities in certain organs such as lungs, brain and in body-fluid such as blood, lymph, saliva and digestive juices. All these organs including the brain work in a better way if provided with the adequate amount of water.

Water helps transport the chemical substances produced by the brain that carry its messages to different parts of the body. Thus, if you want your brain to work efficiently, consume a lot of water. You must drink 8-10 glasses of water daily. *Are you feeling tired physically or mentally and/or are sweating profusely?* Having water would immediately replenish your energy.

Let me tell you some more advantages. Water maintains the normal volume of fluids such as blood and lymph by diluting it to the required consistency. It regulates our body temperature and removes the toxic substances from the body through urine, sweat and letting our brain work properly. Not only that, it also makes our skin more supple and elastic. *Isn't it an easy way to maintain both brain and body beautiful?* Besides this, water also increases the movements of intestines thus facilitating formation and passing soft stools. Thus if our digestive system works properly, we have enough energy for our vital organs to work efficiently, thereby enabling our brain also to function marvellously by storing and recalling the information in a better way.

So, keep your water-bottle always with you so that whenever you need water, it is with you. If you are sitting for your studies, keep the bottle on your table and drink frequently. You can also take your water-bottle to the examination hall.

Keyword: Water

32

Must Break the Night's Fast—Have Breakfast

Having a proper breakfast improves your work performance and thinking ability. Several studies have been conducted regarding this and it was found that the participants performed better in memory-related tests when they took the exams after having breakfast than the ones who did not have.

Even if you are in a hurry and can't prepare breakfast for yourself, don't skip your breakfast. You can have some fat free milk, juice, dry fruits or cookies, etc. That will ensure right glucose level in your blood which energizes your body and brain so as to perform in a better way.

One must have the important meal of the day—breakfast.

Keyword: Morning meal

33

Memory Fruit

Apples are rich in Iron as well as another element called Boron which helps maintain the normal brain activity.

Studies have proved that increasing the intake of Boron from 0.25-3.5 mg daily improves the short term memory performance. You can get much of it in apples, grapes, peaches, cherries, carrots, potatoes and cinnamon.

An apple a day keeps the doctor away and places your memory at the right way.

Keyword: Apple

34

Figurative Thinking

Suppose you are studying about the functioning of the heart and lungs. While making notes, one way is to describe each and every organ and its working while another is to simply draw a sketch. This is known as diagrammatic thinking.

Let us say that a circle is representing the heart and the two oval shapes are representing the lungs which are inside a larger figure representing the body.

Now, show the blue arrows (impure blood) coming out of the heart and going to the lungs where oxygen is taken in and the carbon dioxide is expelled. Then, draw the red arrows (pure blood) back to the heart and from there to the body. If you want to illustrate it further, you can break the circle into four parts showing left and right upper auricles and lower ventricles.

The same thing can be done with maps, charts, etc. The idea is to begin with the most simple bits of details and adding step-by-step on to it no matter how you lay out the information or what the shape you assign.

Think in the form of dots and lines or circles and arrows instead of thinking in words or phrases.

Keyword: Sketch

35

Self Talk

To avoid distraction of your mind and wandering off of your thoughts here and there, try speaking to yourself in order to help focus attention thus making it easier to recall. For example, when you are parking your car, say near a market, get out of the car and start talking to yourself as you walk through the lanes. Describe where you are keeping the keys of your car, what you are going to do, which shops you are walking past and what the place looks like.

When you are through with your work, turn your description around and walk through it in reverse. You will easily locate your parked car.

It is easier to recall the place where you are keeping something or where you have left something only if you consciously make your mind aware of that.

This will also help you remember whether you have taken medicine or vitamins or whether you have already given something to somebody or even if you have kept your file or book or lunch box in your bag or such type of other activities which otherwise may slip from your mind. Verbalize your actions as well as thoughts so as to remember them.

Keyword: Verbalization

36

Potential Study Time

According to the time of going to sleep and getting up, people have different levels of alertness at different hours. The person who goes to bed very late and is a late riser is mentally sharp at quite different times than the fellow who is early-to-bed, early-to-rise kind.

Depending upon how much good sleep you get at night, when and what you eat during the day and also your activity level, the peak time of alertness as well as its length may vary.

Each person has his own cycle of alertness. If you want to make full use of your potential, you must find your own peaks. All you have to do is jot down the timings when you feel fresh and invigorated, and also the period when you are most sluggish. Take note of it for a few days. You will observe a pattern between your clear-headedness and muddle-headedness. You will find it easier to do any mental or creative work or to perform some memory task effortlessly when your energy reserves are at their highest. You can, thus, re-schedule your work accordingly so as to take maximum advantage of your capacity.

Optimize memorization by figuring out maximum alertness.

Keyword: Peak alertness time

37

Creative Debating Game

Ask your friend who is willing to debate on some current controversial issue to write down as many points as possible either supporting or opposing the issue. You jot down the other side of the argument. Now discuss it giving reasons.

If you try to argue both the sides of a particular issue, you will strengthen and improve your logical thinking. During this process, you exercise your mind and hence make it sharp and focused.

To help improve your long-term memory you can call your friend again and discuss the same issue all over again but this time from his perspective without looking at those written points. This will also benefit you in improving your verbal skills.

Strengthen your logic and sharpen your memory by entering into reasoned argument—debate.

Keyword: Debate

38

Memory Signals

An age-old method of giving yourself reminders by tying a thread around your wrist still holds good. But, supposing you don't have a thread at that moment, then you should use other techniques as described below.

Some people turn around their wedding rings if they are unable to write it down due to some important work they are doing at that time or the pencil and paper is not at hand or they got up in the middle of the night due to this anxiety.

Set alarm clocks in home or office at particular times, write 1 on the mirror with chalk, leave yourself a reminder on your answering machine, etc.

Keyword: Reminders

39

Caffeine—The Memory Blaster

Small amounts of caffeine intake, say a cup or two of coffee daily, may activate your short-term memory but only when it is taken at the time while you are feeling low and sluggish. It is useful to take it in the morning when you really need to get going.

If you are already feeling active, don't overstimulate yourself by consuming coffee because that may hamper your memory.

Caffeine affects serotonine, the chemical messenger in the brain which helps to improve the short-term memory.

The source of caffeine is not only coffee but also most of the teas, carbonated sodas such as colas, coffee-flavoured ice-creams and yogurt.

So one must keep in mind the possible impact these products may have on one's memory before consuming them.

Depending upon what time you are taking a cup of coffee, it may boost or jeopardize your memory.

Keyword: Caffeine

40

Munch between the Meals

If you feel lethargic and your performance level is going low, try having the mid-afternoon snack. This will improve your performance and memory.

Many a time, we feel a dip in our enthusiasm to work after a few hours of lunch.

Have some fresh fruits like banana, apple, orange or some vegetable salads, yogurt or curd, juices or even flakes and cookies, etc. Besides keeping you healthy, it will invigorate your brain.

Your body and brain would feel energetic if you take snacks in between.

Keyword: Snacks

41

The Deep Breath Method

If you are feeling nervous, take a few deep breaths to curb your wandering thoughts. This technique is mostly used just before going up to the stage by the performing artistes, actors and public speakers.

Method

Sit in a comfortable position, letting loose your arms and legs as well as neck and shoulders. Keeping your mouth closed, inhale deeply without making a hissing sound from your nose until your lungs are completely filled with air. In this process, bulge your stomach out to give full space to the lungs. Now let the air remain in for a little while. Then exhale slowly through your nose until all of the air is expelled and your lungs are completely empty. The ideal ratio of inhalation to retention vs exhalation is 1:4:2. But one can change it according to one's capacity, e.g., 1:2:1 or so. This is called *pranayam*.

It is a known fact that memory is at its best when the mind is relaxed. To achieve this relaxation, *pranayam* or simply deep breathing is recommended. *Pranayam* will surely help you to recall names, faces, places and other vital information in a better way.

Keyword: *Pranayam*

42

How to Develop Mental Storage Places for Things

You Need to Remember

Here are the names of 20 objects found in most homes. Think of the ones in your own home and imagine them in this order:

In your kitchen	In your bathroom
1. Sink	11. Bath-tub
2. Stove	12. Lavatory
3. Utensils	13. Shelf
4. Table	14. Mirror
5. Refrigerator	15. Towel
In your living room	**In your bedroom**
6. Telephone	16. Bed
7. Easy chair	17. Book rack
8. Lamp	18. Waste-basket
9. TV set	19. Curtain
10. Poster	20. Alarm clock

Read this list over and mentally see each one of these familiar objects in your own home. Next, associate them in a sequence. For example, in your kitchen, there are 5 items. In your living room there are also five items, numbered from 6 to 10. In your bathroom, the bath-tub stands for number 11, the shelf stands for number 13, and the towel stands for number 15. In your bedroom, the bed stands for number 16, the curtain stands for number 19, and the alarm clock stands for number 20.

Now, I'm going to show you how to use your imagination to associate images of things on a shopping list with the pictures of those things in your home which are so familiar to you. When you follow these instructions, you will prove to yourself that you do have an imagination and that you do have the ability to remember.

Here is a shopping list. In a moment I will explain how to remember it by associating each item on this list with the objects in your home.

1. Pen
2. Soap
3. Pencil
4. Flower
5. Cassette
6. Paint
7. Torch
8. Potato
9. Belt
10. Bag
11. Juice
12. Onions
13. Lock
14. Knife
15. Cream
16. Cycle
17. Shirt
18. Washing powder
19. Playing cards
20. Match box

Please follow my instructions carefully. I want you to see each of these pictures with your imagination. It may sound "screwy", but do this exercise. It is of tremendous importance in developing your memory.

1. You are storing *pen* in your kitchen sink. **See it now!**
2. You are washing the dirty *stove* with *soap*. **Visualize it**.
3. See yourself using *pencil* instead of fork kept in utensil while eating food.
4. Visualize a table and see yourself engaged in its decoration with colourful *flowers*. **Have a look at it**.
5. See, the deep fridge of the refrigerator full of cassettes.
6. See, you are *painting* your old black telephone instrument into glittering red. **See it now!**
7. Visualize that you are replacing one of the broken legs of the *chair* with a yellow coloured big *torch*.
8. Mentally, see that you are placing a *potato* instead of a bulb in the bulb-holder of the *lamp*.
9. Picture that you are buckling with a *belt* the expensive *TV set* of your house with a bed so that it may not be taken away by thieves.
10. Visualize your school *bag*. One day in the school, when you open the bag, you find the bag full of posters instead of books. **Look at it now!**
11. See yourself bathing in the *bath-tub* with *lemon juice*. Try to feel the taste of it!
12. Your *lavatory* filled with *onions*. You're peeling them there and your tears fill the bowl. **Look at it now!**

13. Lock your *shelf* mentally with a gigantic lock. See it colourfully.
14. See yourself cutting the mirror into different designs with a big and sharp *knife*. See the handle of the knife in your right hand.
15. See your *towel* covered with *cream*, shelf dripping with cream! **See it now!**
16. You are scared of the road. So you are learning cycling on the *bed*. **Visualize it!**
17. Picture that you are placing *shirts* of different colours in the *book rack* since there is no space in the cupboard.
18. Your *waste-basket* is filled with washing powder. **See it now!**
19. To avoid others know that you have a passion for *playing cards*, you are covering the room all over with *curtains* before beginning the game.
20. Picture your *alarm clock*. Now see match-stick instead of the hour and the minute hands of the alarm clock.

Now write down what you saw with each of these items:

1. Sink_____   11. Bath-tub_____
2. Stove_____   12. Lavatory _____
3. Utensil _____   13. Shelf _____
4. Table _____   14. Mirror _____
5. Refrigerator _____   15. Towel _____
6. Telephone _____   16. Bed _____
7. Easy chair _____   17. Book rack _____
8. Lamp _____   18. Waste-basket _____
9. TV _____   19. Curtain _____
10. Poster _____   20. Alarm clock _____

Stop now and think a few minutes about what you have just done, at first this seemed strange to you. However, you have succeded in associating a picture representing an object on your shopping list with a picture of something you couldn't forget because of your familiarity with it. This method of associating pictures representing items of shopping list with items in your household may also be applied to memorising the points in a sales talk or a speech. Think of how much more confidence you will have when you know you can't possibly forget what you want to say on any occasion! Incredibly simple, isn't it?

Keyword: Permanent storage place

43

Delivering Speech without Notes

How do you feel about speaking in front of a group of people? If you are like many others, you won't be too keen on the idea! No wonder, the natural response is fear! The fear of forgetting the speech.

One alternative the people go for is using a manuscript.

And what is wrong with using a manuscript and reading these thoughts which you have carefully placed on the paper?

My answer is that everything is wrong with a manuscript. In the first place, the contact between the speaker and audience, which is most vital for the success, is missing.

How Do You Deliver a Speech without Notes?

Solution: Say you are to deliver a speech on "Qualities of leadership".

Step I: We must gather and we must review our material.

Step II: We must classify this material, and we must choose when to use introduction, the body of the speech, and the conclusion.

Step III: Select the keywords (also read chapter: *Learning long theory—the keyword method*). Arrange the keywords in the same order as it is in the formal speech.

Say the keywords for the speech are:

1. Unwavering courage
2. Self-control
3. A keen sense of justice
4. Definiteness of plans
5. Definiteness of purpose
6. The habit of doing more
7. A pleasing personality
8. Sympathy and understanding
9. Mastery of details
10. Willingness to assume full responsibility

11. Cooperation.

Step IV: Now look/associate these 11 keywords with the first 11 mental storage places (See chapter: *How to develop mental storage places for things*).

For example, let's say we want to remember the fourth point of the speech "The habit of doing more".

Associate it with the fourth item "Table" (in this case).

That we can do just by thinking that a good leader working round the clock sitting on a *Table*.

Don't forget that a good speaker entails practice and don't expect a perfect speech in the first attempt.

But in this chapter I have given you the basic tools you need.

If you use the "Mental storage place" method properly, rest assured that you will be able to speak on your own whenever the opportunity arises.

Keyword:	Mental notes

44

The Weaker Side

Using your nondominant hand to open the door to your house might unlock a stifled memory.

Have you ever tried to write your signature with your nondominant hand? Remember how hard you had to focus to get even your first name down on the page. By struggling through an activity that normally comes very easily to you, you are activating under-used pathways in your brain that are just waiting to be tapped.

Pick any activity that you naturally do with one hand or the other: brushing your teeth, buttoning a shirt, tying your shoes, dealing cards. When you do it with the opposite hand, the brain registers the immediate contrast to your normal *modus operandi*. Opposing brain hemispheres, normally unchallenged when doing this task, are activated by the sensory and motor information sent by that different hand or foot which means major gains in brain circuit development.

Try to incorporate several nondominant hand tasks into your daily habits. Like any lifestyle change, you may not feel immediate results, but they will gradually accrue over time.

Naturally, though this challenge is just for risk-free tasks, I'd be a little cautious about using your nondominant hand for certain things. You don't want to cut steaks or use power tools or chain saw.

·Keyword:	Left hand

45

Charge Your Brain by Visiting a New Spot

Seeking out and visiting a special spot in nature can improve your memory by helping you to increase your focus, to relax, and to sharpen your observational skills.

One issue with memory is divided attention. If you take time in nature to recharge your batteries, you will feel clearer and your memory is likely to increase.

Find a spot in nature that you connect with preferably within walking distance of your home or work.

The spot you choose could be on a rock near a lake, in a small stand of woods, or even in a quiet park. Try to spend at least half-hour there once a week, and don't take anything that might distract you, such as a book or a personal stereo.

Let your senses deliver messages to you by using "soft eyes", not focusing too strongly on any one element. Think about how perceptions sharpen as you spend more time in your spot: Do you notice the sweetness of honey suckle, the colour of sunlight through leaves, or the harmony of singing birds?

"Emotional old business" will fade away and you will become more focused and alert. Memory is tied into being grounded and centered and living in your body. Immersion in nature helps to create a profound sense of balance and physical awareness."

Keyword:	New place

|46|

Go out of Routine

Just about any habit can get a bit mind numbing. In order to keep your wits sharp, it's crucial to shake up your brain a little bit.

You don't have to quit your job every year or move across the country to get the change of pace your brain is hungry for. A few alterations a day can give your brain enough stimulating charge to brighten that light bulb in your head. By changing your routines you're moving away from relying on a set of well-worn mental paths, always looking for refreshing new opportunities to dampen the daily humdrum—rearranging your furniture, driving a new route to work, wearing your watch on the opposite wrist. The visual change will shift your mind out of automatic mode and help forge new connections in the brain.

These changes may not help you remember 50 names instantly or prompt you to recall a huge text but they do enhance overall brain fitness. Varying routines allow you to have a larger repertoire of possible avenues for information to flow through your brain. You will have a larger network to rely on for greater powers of association, greater creativity, and more flexibility in the way you think.

Keyword: Out of routine

47

Memory Power of Smell

To preserve the vivid memory of an experience, link it to a scent.

Think of scent as a memory preservative. Having a specific odour that you repeatedly use in the same setting will help tap into your brain's powerful capability to make links and association.

Smell is our most potent sense when it comes to memory. Certain neural pathways run straight from your nose to the hippocampus, the centre of learning and memory in your brain.

Unlike other senses, which have to go through a bunch of relay stations in the brain, smell has a direct line. It is like the red telephone in the president's office that's directly linked to Moscow.

You can tag events in your life by tying them to a fragrance. For example, bake the same buns when you're having the family over for Christmas every year. Peel an orange right before you dial a friend's phone number. Light a vanilla-scented candle whenever you do crossword puzzles.

By invigorating your odour universe and linking smells to experiences, you can send them straight to your long-term memory.

Keyword: Smell memory

48

Memory for Numbers

Do you want to remember a phone number without looking it up? It may be as simple as thinking of your anniversary or your grandmother's birthday.

You can remember numerical sequences of any length by using catchy reminders. If you want to remember a three-digit number, for instance, transform it into a time. So, 235 becomes 2.35 p.m. Then, to further hardwire it into your memory, associate that number with what you are generally doing at that time of day, such as taking a coffee break or watching your favourite talk show.

Break a longer number down into smaller, more memorizable parts. So, 402,111 becomes 40, 21, 11, which could be your age, the legal drinking age in your state, and your lucky number. You can also translate a number into a word using your telephone keypad. So 56,425,377, for instance, becomes "knickers".

Keyword: Number association

49

Effective Sleep for Effective Study

Should I study late in the night or should I develop an early morning study habit? How many hours of sleep is sufficient for a student? Is cutting down of sleep time really helpful during exams? Should I go for an afternoon nap?

We must know the effective answers to the above questions to make our studies effective. Consider the following points to understand the importance of sleep in studies.

Sleep Produces Necessary Protein

Not all parts of the brain are at rest during sleep. Electrical activity, oxygen, consumption and energy expenditure in certain parts of the brain actually increase. During this extra neural activity, proteins are manufactured by nerve cells. These proteins help store cellular memories. It is important that you get enough sleep time to allow such protein production to occur because part of the wear and tear of daily life is the continual breakdown of the cellular proteins. If the protein of the brain were to delay without being replaced, all memory would gradually be lost. Sleep thus serves to retain memories through protein replacement which counteracts the continual wear and tear.

Sleep Reorganizes Information

Sleep helps us sort out the load of recent information we have acquired during the day. Everything we see, hear, smell, taste or touch bombards us with an immense wealth of information. Sleep processes the information that we have gathered throughout the day into a convenient plan of neural storage. So never compromise with the amount of sleep. We must have an appropriate amount of sleep. The required amount of sleep varies from individual to individual and depends on the amount of physical and mental activities one had during the day and also the amount of food intake. Generally, the amount of sleep lies between 6-8 hours for students. Also remember that losing sleep, we lose much of our ability to transfer the day's information into long-term memories.

Afternoon Nap

An afternoon nap means two fresh mornings in 24 hours. After you have done your morning's writing and the brain swimming with facts, a nap of 30-45 minutes is required to recharge the brain. Even if the nap leaves you physically out of touch for a while, your mind is sharper and more capable of redirecting your efforts. If you have a job in which an afternoon nap is not possible all is not lost that's because you actually may not need to blank out to take the benefits of the afternoon nap. A brief meditation or a quiet period of time away from the normal influx of information may allow your brain to do the necessary filing to sharpen your memory.

Overcoming Sleeplessness

A few simple guidelines are effective if you have trouble getting to sleep at night.
   1. *Evaluate your caffeine intake*: A cup of coffee or tea after dinner or late night is a serious offender. Continual consumption of caffeine during the day can also build up levels that your body may not remove during bed time.
   2. *Avoid high protein food*: If you have sleeping trouble avoid consumption of high protein food shortly before going to bed. The protein breaks down and releases amino acids that competes with tryptophan and prevents its entry into the brain and robs you of natural brain relaxation process. (Tryptophan relaxes the brain and helps you sleep.)
   3. *Maintain fixed sleep routine*: Sleeping problem may arise by frequently changing the sleeping time. Maintain a particular time of getting in and out of bed.

Ends Are More Productive

It is the characteristic of the brain to retain the first and the last information better than the information given in between. When we are attending a lecture or a seminar, we remember the first information and the last much more clearly than the thing in between. Similar is the case while watching movies. The late one hour before the sleep and an hour just after getting up from the bed is the most productive time. Always use those two productive times of the day for studies. Preferably if you have something to revise, utilize the last one hour of the day (one hour before sleep). The brain is fresh to accept any new thought. So to learn any new topic, use the first one hour after getting up from the bed.

Keywords:	Protein, afternoon nap, reorganize, fixed routine, ends

50

Your Imagination Can Make It Happen

The subconscious mind cannot differentiate between what is real and what we believe is real.

I have collected several true stories to support the above statement.

Proof I

"Man Freezes to Death in Refrigeration Car." The 1964 headline was hardly startling, but the circumstances were. A man had been trapped inside the refrigerator car as the door accidentally slammed on him. When he was found, he had all the physical symptoms of having frozen to death. Yet the refrigeration unit was switched off and at no time had the temperature been at or even close to freezing. He believed he was going to freeze—and his mind had produced the physical effect to create hypothermia and freeze him to death.

Proof II

Dr. Cheureul, a researcher, spoke quietly to his subject, who was holding a pendulum over a straight line on a piece of paper. "Keep it as steady as you can," he instructed, "although you will find that the pendulum is bound to swing up and down the line because of earth's gravitational pull."

After a few minutes, the pendulum began to swing quietly, although the reason Cheureul gave was absolutely bogus. There was no reason for the pendulum to swing other than the subconscious suggestion that it would.

Proof III

Dr. Rosenthal, a California based psychologist, administered IQ tests to a public school class. He totally ignored the results, but nevertheless divided the class into two groups. The first group, he informed the teacher, was considerably brighter than the second. There was in fact no difference. The children were never told about his conclusions and the teacher was told to treat all the pupils equally.

Eight months later, the grades of the two arbitrarily classified groups were compared. The first group had grades 28 per cent better than the second group and their IQ actually measured higher! Without one word being said, the teacher had managed to communicate, quite subconsciously, a higher expectation of the first group and a lower expectation of the second group, all without the subjects even knowing of it. The teacher had created a better learning environment for the favoured group, and it worked.

Proof IV

Students in a Bulgarian class were asked to memorize a poem. Another identically matched class was also asked to memorize the same item, but this time they were told that the author was a famous and respected poet. The second group remembered 60 per cent more than the first group, in the same time period. The authority of the author suggested it was important to learn.

We act not according to what things really are but according to what we expect them to be, believe them to be, imagine them to be. "Imagination", said Napoleon, "rules the world". He should have known, for he actually rehearsed every battle he ever fought in his mind weeks before the event, going over his own tactics, visualizing the enemy defences, their reaction, and the terrain. Napoleon was 105 years ahead of his time.

So, if you really want to make it (your goal) happen, first make it happen in your imagination.

Try to rehearse the whole process as clearly and as often as possible.

| **Keyword:** | Mind power |

51

The 2-Minute Stress Buster Chart

Six Steps for Instant Relief from Stress

Stress reduces our efficiency and badly affects our studies. Next time you are in stress, consider these six points for instant relief:

1. According to research, worry makes you tense and nervous and affects the nerves of your stomach and actually changes the gastric juices of your stomach from normal to abnormal and often leads to stomach ulcers. *"Those who do not know how to fight worry, die young."*
   Dr. Alexis Carrel
   This is one reason for not worrying.

2. One of the worst features of worry is that it destroys our ability to concentrate. When we worry, our mind jumps here and there and everywhere and we lose all power of decision. However, when we force ourselves to face the worst and accept it mentally, we then eliminate all these vague imaginations and put ourselves in a position in which we are able to concentrate on our problem.
   This is second reason for not worrying.

3. *Do this*: Analyze the situation fearlessly and honestly and figure out what the worst could happen as a result of failure. After that calmly devote your time and energy in improving upon the worst which you have already accepted mentally.

4. Carefully read the sentence given below:
   A man is not hurt so much by what happened, as by his opinion of what happened.
   Now follow this unique technique of changing our opinion and mood instantly.
   Action seems to follow feeling, but actually action and feeling go together and by regulating the action which is

under the more direct control of our will, we can indirectly regulate the feeling, which is not.

So, act as if you are happy, speak and walk cheerfully as if you were already cheerful, if possible, even dance for a moment.

Remember the words of Abraham Lincoln: "*Most folks are about as happy as they make up their mind to be.*"

5. *I had the blues because I had no shoes, until upon the street, I met a man who had no feet.*

    Read this every morning and you will never have worries for the things you do not have.

6. *Visualization technique*: Keep a mental storage of the *happier moments* of your life you have experienced. Next time you are tense, go back to your happier days by visualizing yourself in that moment. Try to feel the pleasant atmosphere and music of appreciation of your happier moments.

    We are not what we think we are but what we think, we are.

So next time you are in stress, just refer to this for instant relief.

Keyword: Stop worrying

52

Placebo—The Dummy Pill

It is well known that physicians regularly use placebos, sugar pills or pills with absolutely no real medical power. The patients, however, are told that the pills are powerful medicaments. Countless studies have proved the high effectiveness of these "mind only" medications.

In a 1979 study, patients with severely bleeding ulcers were split into two groups. One was told that they were taking a new drug that would bring immediate relief. The second were told that they were taking an experimental drug, but no much was yet known about its effects. The same drug was administered to both groups: 75 per cent of the first group improved and 25 per cent of the second group. The only difference was the patients' expectations. At Harvard University, Dr Beecher researched pain in postoperative patients. Some were administered morphine and some a placebo. The morphine controlled the pain in 52 per cent of the patients who received it, the placebo controlled the pain in 40 per cent of the patients. In other words, the placebo was 75 per cent as effective as the morphine. The brain, expecting the pain relief, actually triggered the production of endorphin, the naturally produced opiate chemicals that block the neuro transmitters which allow the sense of pain to register on the brain.

Mind Mechanism

Many researchers are now convinced that a good proportion of the benefit derived from real medication is received from the placebo or "halo" effect. Since everyone, including the doctor, knows that extensive testing goes into new drugs, when one is released for use, the doctor expects it to work, the patient expects it to work—and it does work. A placebo works because the subconscious mind finds ways of bringing about what you imagine, and believe, will happen.

Because of the undoubted power of the mind to produce healing or, indeed, sickness in the patient, doctors worldwide are more and more moving toward holistic medicine. Holistic merely means (w)holistic—treating the whole patient—not just his body, but his mind too. In one of the most dramatic proofs of the power of mental attitude over recovery rates, 152 cancer patients at the Travis Air Base in California were rated by their doctors. Without exception the patients with positive expectations had far more successful recovery rates. In fact, only two out of the negative attitude patients showed any response to treatment at all, so much so that the physician in charge was able to state that, "a positive attitude toward treatment was a better predictor of response to treatment than was the severity of the disease."

The above examples illustrate the power of the imagination to suggest behaviour and attitude changes. In some instances, that power was brought about by auto-suggestion; the mind voluntarily created its own reality. In other instances, the suggestion was from an external source. Someone had "put the idea in the subject's heat."

Keyword: Dummy pill effect

53

The Final Checklist for Exams

You might see the examination sheet on the noticeboard or your teacher might refer to the examination paper they are preparing. No matter what the stimulus you are likely to respond by quickly counting the number of weeks or days before the start of the exams, when you consider the pre-examination revision period, you are really confronted with the issue of how to use your remaining time most effectively. That time will go flying by, so it is imperative to get your revision into top gear as soon as possible. Consider the following steps:

Organize Yourself

Organize your revision on several different time plans. That is, work out a weekly study plan for each of the final weeks, a daily plan for each of the days and finally, a study session plan for the next few hours. With this three time plan, you can see how each day's progress relates to your overall task.

Time Effectiveness

Most students know when they function at peak effectiveness. Some people are morning workers, while others find they are most effective in the evening or the night. Given that you are probably going to study at any available hour of the day before your examinations, you might want to consider what subjects you will be studying in your high and low periods. Use your high and low period of the day to gain and maintain momentum.

Stop Worrying

In spite of your positive start, you may find worries sneaking into your learning effort. If this is the case, stand up and turn away momentarily from your desk, take a few deep slow breaths and then return to your study. Standing and breathing deeply—be sure to breathe slowly.

Think Positively

Assert your positive attacks upon your revision by working on a card with the words: Yes I can do it! Place the card in front of your books and notes so that you can see the words every time you glance up.

Study Breaks

Take frequent but short breaks from your studying, as mental and physical fatigue will begin to wear you down. While you are trying to absorb a lot of work, your mind will need these short rests so that you can maintain the pace. Just getting up from the desk, walking around the room several times and then sitting down again can be a sufficient break.

Focused Reading

Focus upon the major points in your revision. Time is very limited and you will have to be very selective about how you are spending it. There is no time for learning minute and trivial details. At the eleventh hour, you can expect to master or revise only the major points.

Avoid Excessive Stimulants

Beware of stimulants such as coffee, tea and stay-awake tablets. You probably will find that your nervous system is already in top gear and the last thing you need is additional stimulation. Too much caffeine in your body under tense cramming conditions can produce negative effects.

Keyword: Checklist

54

The π Method

There's a good reason why most telephone numbers in the world are between six and ten digits. We humans aren't very good at remembering large chunks of information. In fact, we typically have trouble recalling anything more than 7 or more distinct pieces of information at a time. You might remember that there were ten cars parked in a lot, but if they were all different, you would probably be hard pressed to remember each one's colour and its order in line.

Creative Abilities

Here, your creative abilities can come to your rescue. The value of π can be a perfect example of handling the random digits.

1. π = PI.E

Hold the above sign up to a mirror (please do it now).

2. Let's say you want to memorise the value of pie up to six places after decimal.

π = 3.141593

Just remember, "How I wish I could calculate pie".

Here, the number of letters in each word equal the digits of π.

3. To remember:

π = 3.14159265348979

Just remember, "How I would like an alcoholic drink of course after the heavy lectures involving quantum mechanics."

Using the advanced mnemonics method, I memorised the value of π up to 4200 digits after decimal and can repeat it in forward, reverse order and also I can tell which is the digit at 3456th or 2945th place, etc. after the decimal. (for which my name is there in Limca Book of Records, 2001 edition).

| Keyword: | Word number |

55

Link Method for Formulae

"I often confuse by thinking whether it is $\cos^2\theta$ or $\cos\theta^2$? Whether it is $a^2b - b^2a$ or $b^2a - a^2b$. Whether it is $4\cos^3A - 3\cos A$ or $3\cos A - 4\cos^3A$.

These are some of the very common complaints which I usually hear from students. Even the slightest mistake in recollecting a formula may result in a completely wrong answer. Now the basic question is:

How to avoid all these confusions?

The Formula Method

Step I: Maintain a separate formulae book and try to update it every time you come across any new set of formulae.

Step II: Categorize the formulae.

Type I: Formulae to be learnt by understanding, for example
$|Z_1 + Z_2| \leq |Z_1| + |Z_2|$
$||Z_1| - |Z_2|| \leq |Z_1 - Z_2|$ Triangle Inequality

Those who have studied triangle inequality know that such kind of formulae should be understood and are not to be learnt by rote.

Type II: Formulae to be learnt by rote, for example:

$$\cos 2A = \frac{1 - \tan^2 A}{1 + \tan^2 A}$$

$$\cos 3A = 4\cos^3 A - 3\cos A$$

Step III: Try to figure out the part in a formula where you may get confused.

For example, whether $\cos 2A$ is $\dfrac{1 - \tan^2 A}{1 + \tan^2 A}$

or $\dfrac{1 + \tan^2 A}{1 - \tan^2 A}$

Or written cos3A is
$$4\cos^3 A - 3\cos A \text{ or } 3\cos A - 4\cos^3 A$$
Step IV: Try to make that confusion outstanding.
For example:

$$\boxed{\cos^2 A} = \frac{1-\tan^2 A}{1 + \tan^2 A}$$

$$\boxed{\cos 3A} = \boxed{4\cos^3 A} - 3\cos A$$

By connecting it like this, you have given your confusion a visual form.

Keyword: Link confusion

56

Clue Method—For Learning Foreign Languages

The salesman who speaks the language of his prospective customer has such an enormous advantage over his competitor who does not that there can hardly be any doubt about the comparative success of their respective business trips.

What is the easiest way to learn a foreign language?
Answer: The clue method.

For example, if you want to learn that the French word *jeu* means *game*, you can do it simply by thinking of *joy* as a link which is similar in sound of the French word *jeu* and associate by thinking getting joy out of playing a game. This kind of thinking is sufficient to recall the foreign word whenever we need it. Moreover, experience shows that after a while the linking word will vanish from our mind and the association between the French and the English word will become so strong that we shall recall the other directly and without the help of the linking words.

Example 1: The French word *lagare* means *railway station*. We can learn it by simply thinking of *line guard* which is similar in sound of lagare. Now link it to the meaning by thinking *a line guard of railway station*.

Example 2: The Spanish word *el libro* means *book*.
Step I: A similar sounding word for *el libro* could be library.
Step II: Connecting the word *library* with the actual meaning *book* by thinking *library* is a collection of *books* in organized manner for sharing.

Example 3: Latin word *poena* means *punishment*.
Step I: Similar sounding word—*peon*.
Step II: Connection—*Peon* got *punishment* for his mischief.

Some more examples from various languages:

English	Linking Word	French
pavement	trot	le trottoir
depth	profound	la profoundeur
body	corporal	le corps
knife	cut	le couteau
foreigner	stranger	un etranger
the back	dorsal	le dos
father	paternal	le pere
mother	maternal	lamere
green	verdant	vert
horse	cavalry	le cheval
flower	florist	la fleur
barn	grain	el granero
narrow	strait	estrecho
sea	marine	el (or la) mar
desk	scribble	el escritorio
book	library	el libra
word	apalver	la palabra
ladder	scale	la escalera
sky	celestial	el cielo
tree	arboreal	el drbol
cloud	nebulous	la nube
world	mundane	el mundo
stone	petrous	la piedra

English	Linking Word	German
water	aqueous	la agua
silver	plate	la plata
mirror	speak	der Spiegel
medicine	arsenic	die Arznei
miracle	wonder	das Wunder
short	curt	kurz
black	swarthy	schwarz
girl	maid	das Madchen
chair	stool	der Stuhl
piano	clavichord	das Klavier
flour	meal	das Mehl
desk	pulpit	das Pult

English	Linking Word	Latin
new	novel	novus
land	territory	terra
field	acre	ager
man	human	homo
war	belligerent	bellum
storm	tempest	tempestas
hand	manual	manus
head	cap	caput

57

Clue Method—For Vocabulary

Vocabulary plays a very important role specially in competitive examinations like MBA, GMAT, etc.

The rules which we have applied to the vocabularies of foreign languages (Read chapter: *Clue method for learning foreign languages*) can likewise be applied to words in English that are unfamiliar to us. Theoretically speaking, it does not make much difference whether we hear a Spanish word or an English word for the first time. If we do not know a particular word, we must do something about it and the best way to remember it is to find a linking word.

Word	Meaning	Link
ablution	washing, cleansing	bluing, or lotion
helot	a slave	It's a hell of a lot to be a slave
hedonism	self-indulgence, devotion to pleasure	plunging head on into pleasure
psoriasis	a skin disease	sores
litigant	one engaged in a lawsuit	little to gain
amanuensis	secretary	manuscript
hegemony	leadership, superiority	hedge (first over the)
flagellate	to whip	flog
conversant	familiar by use of study	conversation (We should hold conversation only about things we are familiar with.)
aver	to affirm positively	verify
apophthegm	a brief statement of a recognised truth	apostle
exculpate	to clear from the imputation of a fault	culprit

Keyword: Clue method

58

Memory Method for General Knowledge and Biological Terms/Definitions

(Must read chapters: *Clue method for learning foreign languages* and *Clue method for vocabulary* before reading this.) Let's say you want to remember that Sofia is the capital of Bulgaria.

We can link Sofia with Bulgaria by just thinking a Bull (garia) is sitting in a sofa (ia).

Country	Capital
Bahrain	Manna

Association: A man(na) in (Bah) rain.

Belgium	Brussels

Association: G.M. cleaning a Bell with Brush (sels).

Cameroon	Yaoonda

Association: A person with a camera (roon) clicking a picture of (Ya) Honda.

Bermuda	Hemilton

Association: Visualize a (He) melting Bermuda. (More silly the association, better is the retention)

Cuba	Havana

Association: A cube (a) in Heaven.

Country	Capital
Dominica	Roseau

Association: You are served Domino's pizza with a Rose.

The same clue method is applicable in learning minerals/industries and places also. For example to learn that the place Katni is known for cement, just think/visualize a **Cat's knee** (Katni) made up of cement.

Place   **Mineral/Industries**
Mysore   Silk
Association: My saree is made up of silk.
Pimpri   Penicillin
Association: To remove pimples, apply Penicillin.

Similarly, this technique is applicable in learning difficult biological words and their definitions.

1. *Buccal cavity*: Mouth cavity by which food is taken inside.
   Association: Visualize yourself buccaling your mouth.
2. *Agglutination*: Clamping together of red blood cells or bacteria as a result of the action of antibodies.
   Association: Clamping very big red blood cells with an egg glue, in a tin.
3. *Cheata*: Bristle-like structure in some animals like earthworms which they use for gripping the soil during locomotion.
   Association: Visualize a Cheeta with bristles all over body and using it for running instead of using legs.
4. *Graft:* Transplantation of an organ or a tissue in animals or plants.
   Association: Grafting with organs.

59

Learning Long Theories— The Keyword Method

One of the common problem among students is learning long theories. Students often complain that they are unable to comprehend even a fraction after the first reading. Often, the mind goes here and there and everywhere except in the theory.
How to concentrate? How to remain focused?
Answer: The keyword method.
Let's understand it step-by-step:
Step: 1 Read and spend a few moments on the heading of the chapter. Try to gather mentally whatever knowldege you can about the heading. For instance, the chapter is "Thermodynamics". The chances are you might not be knowing anything about the term or heading. Even then, try to expect something. Look deeper into the heading. In this case, *Thermodynamics.* *Thermo* means something about heat or I could expect the chapter is all about dynamics of heat. By concentrating and guessing about the chapter and forming an idea even before reading it you are forming a subconscious platform for it.

Your guessing may not be correct every time. Even then, this exercise will help you in developing concentration and positive state for mind for the chapter.

Step 2: Now, read every paragraph (of the given theory with an aim of finding a keyword. Keyword may be defined as the representative word of the whole paragraph. (You might have noticed at the end of every chapter, I have suggested a keyword for the chapter which would help in recollecting the whole chapter).

Step 3: Make a point that you will go to the next paragraph of the chapter only after identifying the keyword of the previous paragraph. This will ensure a perfect focus.

Step 4: Now, if it is a chapter with 15 paragraphs, this means that you have already collected 15 or more keywords. Now, look at the keyword and try to comprehend the whole chapter with it.

Step 5: The next time you revise, keywords will help you revise the chapter faster.

(*Also read chapter: The 'I' factor for perfect concentration*).

| **Keyword:** | Representative word |

60

Remembering Scientific Data

"*Melting point of lead is 327°C or 237°C? Silver at 1950°C or 1590°C? Whether the atomic mass of mercury is 201 or 210 a.m.u.?*"

Students often find it difficult and confusing like this. How to learn all the required melting/boiling points, atomic number/mass, valancies or other standard scientific data?

Phonetic Method

Phonetic method can help you in dealing with all this and that too perfectly.

In this system, the numerals 0 to 9 are represented by specific alphabets. You just have to learn those alphabets with the hints given.

No.	Alphabet	Hints to memorise
1.	t or d	small "t" or "d" has one down stroke
2.	n	Small "n" requires two down strokes
3.	m	m requires three down strokes or the shape of m is similar to 3
4.	r	Four, in majority of languages ends with r. In Hindi, its *Char*, in Latin it's Quatter in Russian it's *Shutter*, etc.
5.	l	In Roman "L" means 50, here small "l" means 5
6.	j or g	The mirror image of j is like 6. The reverse of g is like 6.
7.	k	Two sevens can form a k $K \rightarrow$
8.	f, v	The shape of small "f" (in running handwriting) is like 8
9.	P, b	self explanatory.
0.	S	☼ Sun

Now spend a few more minutes committing all these codes to memory. Let's understand in a step-by-step fashion how to use it in learning that melting point of lead is 327°C.

Step I: Replace every number with a corresponding alphabet.

3	2	7
m	n	k

Step II: Now think of a word consisting of the sound of 'm', 'n' and 'k' in the same order.

Your options   i) MoNKey
 (ii) MaNeka
 (iii) MoNiKa

Step III: Associate any of the option with lead.
Association: MoNKey writing with a LEAD pencil.

Step IV: Visualize it as perfectly as possible.

Next time whenever you require the melting point of lead automatically the word *Monkey* will pop up in your mind and the conversion of 'monkey' will always be 327°C. Obviously, you will ignore the unwanted letters (o, e, y) since they doesn't represent any number. This complete process should not take more than 30 seconds.

Another example: Silver melts at 1950°C.

1	9	5	0
t	b	l	s

The conversion: TaBLeS
Association: Silver Tables.
Visualization: Imagine you study TaBleS made up of Silver.
Example: Atomic mass of mercury 201 a.m.u.

2	0	1
n	s	t

The conversion: A NeST.
Association: Mercury thermometer in a NeST.

You can use this method even to memorize house numbers and telephone numbers. For instance, if you wish to memorise my mobile No.: 9811139474 (Delhi Mobile), obviously you will first ignore 98 since in more of the cases the starting digits of mobile numbers are 98 only.

1	1	1	3	9	4	7	4
t	t	t	m	p	r	k	r
d	d	d	b				

The final conversion: DDT My PaRKeR.

Association: Visualize yourself filling DDT in My PaRKeR (pen).

Keyword: Number image conversion

61

Memory Puzzle

Ask your friend to make some puzzles by jumbling the letters in the words. For example: *ppeal* for *apple*, *wrces* for *screw*, *ptrace* for *carpet*, *tpanl* for *plant*, *trekoc* for *rocket*, etc. Now solve these jumbled words within a prescribed time span.

Another method is asking your friend to make up a random block of letters and numbers like the one shown below.

ODS2KG8A2Y1L39PcJM7FH
BJA4VKNOAECHAM34LZ514S
PYTQ9XLPROPNM3FO2UNIVE
ZXTR51RS2PHSDL9KDP8JLF
ST20LJMNDU378J7DNEPQRS
NDS5L8SJGMLCHANCL52PON

One can use as many sets of letters and numbers. Ask him to set a time limit within which you have to pick several letters or numbers or a combination of both. For example, you may circle every H within 10 seconds.

Circle the chosen figures with the pencil so that it could be erased and the same grid could be used again after a few days, looking for a different set of combinations this time.

One should try to create a new chart of numbers and letters to exercise with so as to improve one's concentration. This exercise should be done at least twice a week or so.

Provide your mind with a mental work out by solving the jumble to improve your attention span and memory.

Keyword: Puzzle

62

Marker Landmark Events

If you are unable to remember the exact date or month or year when you shifted to your new house, try thinking about the other events going on in your lifetime.

Whatever has happened in your life long back did not happen in isolation from the other events. Try taking some clue or marker for certain events that help you focus on your life at that instance. Some major political happenings, sports events, hit movies or popular songs at that time may also help bringing your memory back to a particular time frame.

All you need to recall is to begin thinking of the other details of your life while establishing a certain memory of that period in your mind.

If still unsuccessful, your marker can provide you at least with a time frame that could be used for additional enquiry from family members and friends or additional research if necessary.

Use significant events of your life such as getting a degree or job as memory markers.

Keyword: Major events

63

Learn the Mnemonic Way

A well-crafted acronym can help you recall the most insignificant item on any shopping list.

Take the first letter from the name of each item you're trying to remember, then form those letters into a word. If you need to buy hamburger, tomato, onions, ketchup, olive oil, cabbage and radishes, you have the letters H, T, O, K, O, C and R to work with. It does not seem too promising, does it? Rearrange them a little, and you just have to remember to buy HOTROCK while at the store. The same can be done with errands you need to do (pay the PEC—power, electricity and cable) or things you have to remember at work (do FIRE—filing, invoicing, reading and e-mail).

If you don't have enough letters to make full words then you see a close-matching substitute. LIMPS, for example, is a good substitute for LMPZ because it will probably jog your memory as well, if not better, than a unrelated cluster of consonants (find more in the book).

Keyword: Mnemonic way

64

Smart Memory for Spellings—I

"*I confuse by thinking whether it is `i' before `e' or `e' before `i'"? Whether it is `occassion' or 'occasion' or 'ocassion' ? Principal/ Principle—means rule/head or otherwise?"*

The person with the ability to spell words accurately is one who has a good visual memory. He knows we "read" one English langauge and "speak" another English language. In other words, he doesn't make the mistake of spelling words the way they sound rather than the way they read.

To remedy the spelling mistakes, we have to put our vision back to work. I am going to show you how the visualization principle can keep you out of spelling trouble.

Type I

One wrong letter inserted. Example *calandar* instead of *calendar*.

Remedy: Write the word "calendar" five times but when get to the "e", stop and write it as a capital letter like this *calEndar, calEndar, calEndar, calEndar, calEndar*.

Now you have replaced the careless use of "a" by vivid visualization on capital "E".

You are back visualizing, seeing things as they are with little flip of exaggeration to make the point penetrate.

Type II

Adding an unnecessary letter to the end of the word.
Example, *develope*.
Remedy: Write out the word incorrectly.

Yes, I mean it. Write it wrong but when you finish take your pencil and make a big cross-out mark through the extra "e" like this—*develope develope develope develope*.

Again, you have made the error visual, and just like the

cross bones on the bottle of poison, you have a visual warning.

Type III

Using one of the kind when two are due. Example, ocurrence instead of *occurrence*.

Remedy: Write it out five times. Write the pairs of letters and underscore them. Like this: o<u>CC</u>u<u>RR</u>ence, o<u>CC</u>U<u>RR</u>ence, o<u>CC</u>u<u>RR</u>ence, o<u>CC</u>u<u>RR</u>ene, o<u>CC</u>u<u>RR</u>ence.

Type IV

Forgetting to link a silent letter to another. Example, spelling of *management* without "e".

Remedy: Write it out and draw a circle linking "e" and "g": mana⊙ment, mana⊙ment, mana⊙ment.

Type V

Principle means rule while *principal* means head of an institution.

Memory aid: *principlE* means *rulE* and *princiPAL* is *my PAL*.

A Spelling List of Some of the Troublesome Words:

A	Cite (quotation)	existence
accessible	collateral	exorbitant
accommodate	concession	extension
accrued	consensus	G
acquitted	counterfeit	grammar
across	D	H
allege	develop	harass
allotted	dictionary	height
all right	disappear	hypocrisy
apparel	disappoint	I
athletics	discipline	illegible
audible	dissatisfied	incredible
auxiliary	dissimilar	inoculate
B	E	intercede
benefited	eligible	irresistible
besiege	embarrass	L
bookkeeper	enervate	laboratory
C	equipped	legitimate
calendar	especially	licenee
Cincinnati	exhilarate	loneliness

M
mail chute
maintenance
management
mileage
misspell
momentous
mucilage
N
ninth
noticeable
O
occasion
occurred
occurrence
omission
omitted
optimistic
P
pamphlet

penitentiary
personnel
persuade
precede
preferring
prejudice
principal
procedure
profession
pronunciation
Q
questionnaire
R
recommend
referring
repetition
restaurant
S
seize
sentinel

separate
sergeant
serviceable
site (a place)
strictly
superintendent
supersede
T
tragedy
transient
typing
U
unmanageable
W
welfare
whose
Y
yield

65

Memory Aid to Improve Spellings—II

This is in continuation to the previous chapter where we have shared some memory tips to help us reduce spelling mistakes. We often confuse whether it should be *privilage* or privilege, whether it is *drunkenness* or *drunkeness*, whether it is *truely* or *truly*, whether it is *seizure* or *siezure*, etc.

Here are some more memory techniques to improve upon all this:

Technique I

Step I: Figure out the confusion.
For instance *repitition* or *repetition*

Step II: Make an association with the confused alphabet(s). For instance: *repetition*: To have one *pet*, then another *pet*, and again another *pet*, that is repetition.

Similarly to learn it is *surprise* and not *sarprise* think of "He who is *surprised, surrenders*."

Some more examples:

coolly:	Double the o, double the l. And coolly you will spell.
supersede:	Supersede means set aside.
disappear: and disappoint;	Two partners were disappointed and disappeared.
inimitable:	The table at the party was set in an inimitable way.
recommend:	The Commandant recommends two mariners for promotion.
privilege:	Every legacy is a privilege.
incidentally:	Whether someone is tall or short is purely incidental.
balloon:	The child played with his ball and his balloon, too.

discriminate:	Discriminate against men who are dishonest.
occurrence:	That the current issue of a magazine is sold out is a frequent occurrence.
truly:	"I love you truly" does not always mean for eternity.
assistant:	Nobody wants an ass as assistant,
comparative:	Compared to rats, mice are small.
occasion:	For the occasion, cocoa was served.
necessary:	If you listen carefully, it will not be necessary to say something twice.
grammar:	Don't mar your speech by using poor grammar.
principal:	If you obey school rules, the principal will be your pal.
drunkenness:	The drunkenness of two nobs lasted two nights.
sacrilegious:	What is sacrilegious is also illegal.
parallel:	Two lines run a long way together.
proceed:	Proceed with speed.
pronunciation:	Nuncios and nuns must have good pronunciation.
seizure:	Seizure of enemy installations.
receive:	Receive exclusive information.
conscience:	Justices of the Supreme Court have good consciences.
embarrassed:	Two robbers were embarrassed when they were given two-year sentences.
friend:	End comes at the end.

66

The Number Rhyme Method

This is the first and simplest, effective method of generating mental image. It will help us in generating the first twenty memory codes. In this method we shall take the help of pronunciation of the number to decide its mental image/ code.

Let's start with the number *one*. *One* is similar in pronunciation to the word sun or nun or bun etc.

Now, we need to select any one of them. Let's select sun. So from now onwards our mental image for one is *sun*.

Similarly think something that rhymes with two. It is essential to make the memory image as imaginative, as colorful and as bright as possible. Keep in mind the ten principles of better memory while making image.

For example, for the number 2 we can imagine something similar in pronunciation like zoo or shoe. Our mental image for 3 can be tree or knee.

Let's select one mental memory code each for first 20 numbers.

One	—	sun
Two	—	shoe
Three	—	tree
Four	—	door
Five	—	wife
Six	—	vicks
Seven	—	Heaven
Eight	—	plate
Nine	—	wine
Ten	—	hen
Eleven	—	lemon
Twelve	—	shelf
Thirteen	—	thirsting (mental image—a glass of water)
Fourteen	—	fort in (mental image—a big fort)
Fifteen	—	lifting (mental image—weight lifter lifting weights)

Sixteen	—	sweet sixteen
Seventeen	—	sethin (mental image—a fat seth)
Eighteen	—	Attacking (mental image—scene of a war)
Nineteen	—	Namkeen
Twenty	—	Aunty (mental image—your favourite Aunty)

Go through these 20 mental codes properly and when prepared, appear for the test.

Fill in the blanks with the appropriate codes:

i) Code for 1 is ....
ii) Code for 7 is ....
iii) Code for 19 is ....
iv) Code for 15 is ....
v) Code for 14 is ....
vi) Code for 6 is ......
vii) Code for 10 is ....
viii) Code for 11 is ......
ix) Code for 18 is ......
x) Code for 20 is ......
xi) Code for 4 is ....
xii) Code for 13 is ....
xiii) Code for 16 is ....
xiv) Code for 17 is ......
xv) Code for 9 is ....
xvi) Code for 5 is ......
xvii) Code for 2 is ....
xviii) Code for 12 is ....
xix) Code for 8 is ....
xx) Code for 3 is ......

If your score is sixteen or above, then just revise those mental images which you could not recall.

If your score is below sixteen, you need to read the chapter again.

Once you have memorized all the 20 codes, you are prepared to use it. Go to the chapter seventeen to see one of its uses.

67

How to Use Rhyme Method

The Mental Shopping Test

Everyday, we make mental note of things that must be ordered or replaced. Yet at the end of a day, we forget to attend to several of these things, just because each one in itself is trivial.

Take the problem of the shopping list. If you wait until just before you leave the house to shop to write down what you need, you know what usually happens.

You forget some item— usually the very one you need the most. That means a second trip to the store or frantic telephone call, possibly with delivery charges attached to it. And every now and then, for you are only a human, you arrive at the store to realize that you have left your shopping list on the kitchen table.

The use of the Mental Filing System instead of a written shopping list is the solution to your troubles. You make up your list as you go along, and retain it in your head. You can't leave it on the kitchen table. Errands, groceries, and all needed household supplies are filed at the very moment that you first notice a need for them. If you happen to be scrubbing the bathroom sink when you notice that there is only thin silver of toilet soap left, you file soap at once on your list of key words. You don't have to dry your hands or hunt for a pencil to do this. When the mail comes half an hour later, you remember you need stamps. You immediately hang stamps on its proper keyword and go about your work confident that when you go to shop, everything you need will come to mind automatically, as you call up its keyword.

For the sake of practice, let us take a fairly typical shopping list and see how the items may be fitted reliably on the twenty memory codes, we already know.

1. Shirt
2. Ball
3. Calculator
4. Knife
5. Cake
6. Pepsi
7. Football
8. Soap
9. DDT
10. Stapler
11. Watch
12. Tiffin box
13. Potato
14. Rubber
15. Mirror
16. Butter
17. Belt
18. Bucket
19. Apple
20. Bangles

Let's try to memorize the items with the help of memory codes:

Item 1: Shirt

Memory code 1: Sun
Mental picture : Visualize a shirt with a big sun drawn on it.

Item 2: Ball

Memory code 2 : Shoe
Mental picture : You are unable to wear a shoe since balls are inside.

Item 3: Calculator

Memory code 3: Tree
Mental picture: A calculator tree i.e., tree with lot of calculators hanging.

Item 4: Knife

Memory code 4: Door
Mental picture: See yourself trying to cut the door with knife since it is bolted from inside.

Item 5: Cake

Memory code 5: Wife
Mental picture: Offering cake to wife on her birthday.

Item 6: Pepsi

Memory code 6: Vicks
Mental picture: Applying vicks as you caught cold by drinking lot of cold Pepsi.

Item 7: Football

Memory code 7: Heaven

Mental picture: All the God and Goddesses are playing football.

Item 8: Soap

Memory code 8: Plate
Mental picture: Applying Soap on plate to clean it.

Item 9: DDT

Memory code 9: Wine
Mental picture: Dissolving DDT in wine to purify it.

Item 10: Stapler

Memory code 10: Hen
Mental picture: Stapling hen's beak so that it may not disturb you by cocking.

Item 11: Watch

Memory code 11: Lemon
Mental picture: Free one lemon with every watch.

Item 12: Tiffin box

Memory code: Shelf
Mental picture: Visualize lot of Tiffin boxes lying on a shelf. We can further strengthen the mental picture by thinking that you are trying to adjust a few more.

Item 13: Potato

Memory code: Thirsting (glass of water)
Mental picture: Drinking water in a glass made of potato.

Item 14: Rubber

Memory code: Fort (in)
Mental picture: Sweeper cleaning the wall of fort with rubber.

Item 15: Mirror

Memory code 15: Lifting
Mental picture: A weightlifter is lifting a heavy mirror.

Item 16: Butter

Memory code 16: Sweet sixteen
Mental picture: See yourself buttering a sweet sixteen girl.

Item 17: Belt

Memory code 17: Seth (in)
Mental picture: Robbers tying a Seth with belt.

Item 18: Bucket

Memory code 18: Attacking
Mental picture: Your neighbour is attacking you with a bucket.

Item 19: Apple

Memory code 19: Nun (thin)
Mental picture: Nuns sitting on a heap of apples and also eating the same so that they may gain weight.

Item 20: Bangles

Memory code 20: Aunty
Mental picture: Visualize your Aunty wearing 100 bangles in each hand and doing lot of show off.

Try to recall all the 20 words in the same order and fill in the blanks.

1. ....   2. ....   3. ....
4. ....   5. ....   6. ....
7. ....   8. ....   9. ....
10. ....   11. ....   12. ....
13. ....   14. ....   15. ....
16. ....   17. ....   18. ....
19. ....   20. ....

68

The Number Shape Method

As we have seen, to develop memory codes from 1 to 20 we used the pronunciation/sound of the digits and substituted each of the digit with word rhyming with the particular digit. And also we have just seen one of the numerous uses of the memory codes in the previous chapter.

Now to form memory codes from 21 to 40 we shall concentrate in the shape of the unit digit. For example unit digit of 21 is 1 and the shape of 1 is similar to stick, so the memory code for 21 is stick.

Similarly let's form memory codes for digits from 22 to 40.

Digits	Concentrate on shape of	Mental image
21	1	Stick
22	2	Duck
23	3	Heart
24	4	Chair
25	5	Hook
26	6	Hockey
27	7	Lamp post
28	8	Spectacles
29	9	Lolly pop
30	10	Bat and ball
31	11	Legs
32	12	Knob
33	13	Bow
34	14	Flag
35	15	Cigar pipe
36	16	Elephant trunk
37	17	Bermuda triangle
38	18	Sand watch
39	19	Stapler
40	20	Scooter

Shape of numbers

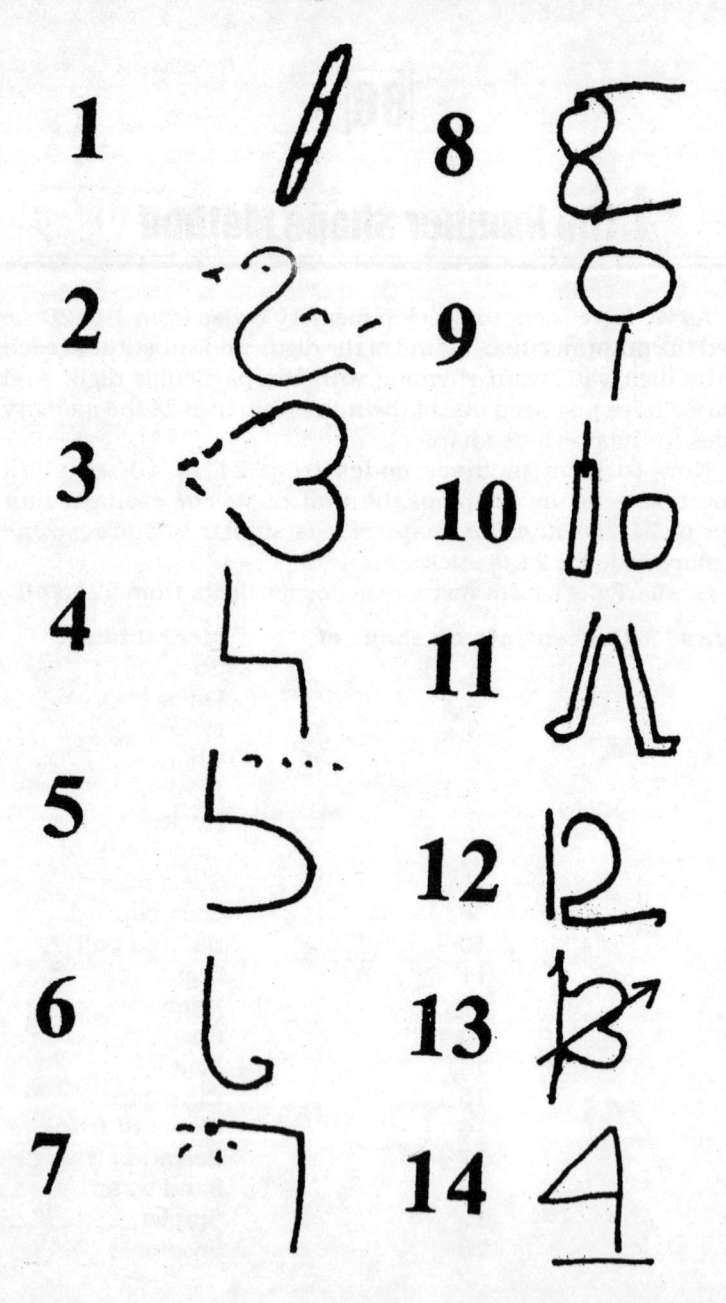

1 · 8 ·
2 · 9 ·
3 · 10 ·
4 · 11 ·
5 · 12 ·
6 · 13 ·
7 · 14 ·

Shape of Numbers Cont...

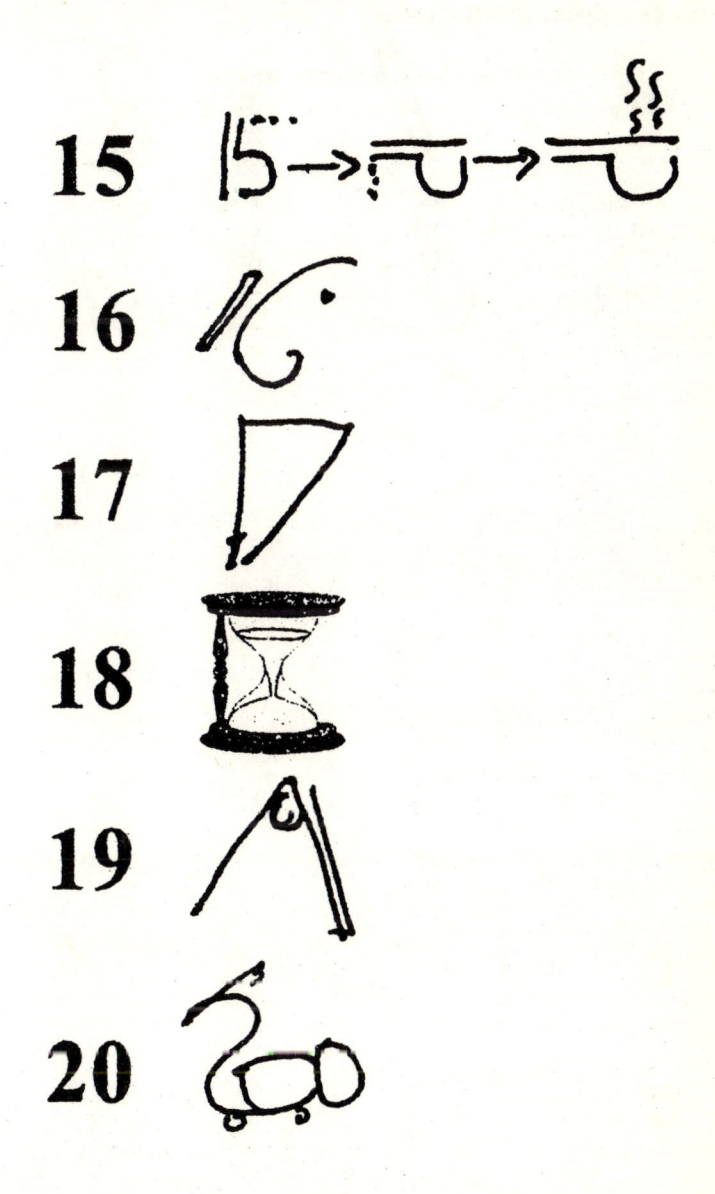

15

16

17

18

19

20

Memorize all the 20 memory codes with the help of the corresponding shape and once you are confident of all the 20 codes, appear for the test.

Fill in the blanks with memory codes.

23.	24.	37. ....
39.	36.	22. ....
25.	29.	32. ....
38.	33.	26. ....
40.	21.	28. ....
27.	30.	35. ....
34.	31.	

69

The Value Method (41-60)

By using this method we shall form memory codes from 41 to 60. Here, we shall concentrate on the VALUE of the unit digit of each of the numbers from 41 to 60 and try to give it an image relevant to the value of that particular unit digit. e.g.

41.— the unit digit is 1.
One means a single entity.
Memory image: President or King of any country could just be 1.
42.— unit digit — 2.
Memory image — couple
43.— unit digit — 3
Memory image: Three monkeys of Gandhiji
44.— Unit digit — 4
Memory image — Four wheels of car.
Similarly image for other number are given in the table.

Number	Concentrate on the value	Mental image
41	1	King
42	2	Couple
43	3	Three monkeys of Gandhiji
44	4	Four wheels of car
45	5	Five fingers
46	6	Eunuch
47	7	Seven Rainbow colours
48	8	Eight legs of Octopus
49	9	Nine Planets
50	10	Ten heads of Ravan
51	11	11 players of football team
52	12	One dozen banana
53	13	13 is an unlucky no.

54	14	14 years of Ram's exile to jungle (*Banvas*)
55	15	15th August is Independence Day
56	16	Sweet (Sixteen) *Note*: Here our mental image cannot be sweet sixteen since we have already used it at No. 16, as here our mental image could just be Sweet.
57	17	Not so sweet mental image: CHILI
58	18	Voter's age
59	19	1900 century (Mental Image: CALENDaR)
60	20	Rs. 20 lakhs lottery ticket.

Memorize the mental image associated with the numbers from 41 to 60 keeping in mind the value of the particular digits.

Once you are finished with the memorizing part attempt the following test:

Q. Fill in the blanks with appropriate mental codes:

47. ....   52. ....   59. ....
60. ....   41. ....   43. ....
48. ....   58. ....   57. ....
42. ....   44. ....   46. ....
53. ....   54. ....   45. ....
55. ....   56. ....   49. ....
51. ....   50. ....

70

The Alphabet Method (61-80)

In this method, we shall generate code for numbers from 61 to 80 by referring to alphabets.

Step 1: Allocate alphabets to digits from 61 to 80.
1st Alphabet A to 61
2nd Alphabet B to 62
3rd Alphabet C to 63
4th Alphabet D to 64
"
"
"
"
"

10th Alphabet J to 70
15th Alphabet O to 75
20th Alphabet T to 80

Step II: Now start with A, think of any word with A as first letter.

The first word, which strikes most of us, is Apple.
So, Apple becomes the code for 61.
Similarly for 62, it could be Ball.
For rest of them, it could be as follows:-

Digits	Concentrate on alphabet	Memory image
61	A	Apple
62	B	Ball
63	C	Cat
64	D	Dog
65	E	Egg
66	F	Fan
67	G	Gun
68	H	Horse
69	I	Ink pot

70	J	Jug
71	K	Kite
72	L	Lion
73	M	Mango
74	N	Nest
75	O	Owl
76	P	Pen
77	Q	Queen
78	R	Radish
79	S	Sea
80	T	Tea

Memorize all the codes from 61 to 80, so that you may be able to give the memory image of the number randomly.

71

The Memorable Event Method (81-100)

The memorable events between year 1981 to 2000 shall serve as a memory image (codes) for the numbers from 81 to 100.
For instance—
One memorable event of year 1981. June 24, 1981, India's first geostationary satellite experimentally launched from FRENCH GUIANA.
The above event would serve as a memory code for 81.
Some selected major events given below which can be used as a memory image for numbers from 81 to 100.

No.	Event	Memory image
81	June 24, 1981:	India's first geostationary experimental telecommunication satellite launched from French...... MEMORY CODE—Satellite
82	Mar 19, 1982:	Ninth Asian games started in New Delhi MEMORY CODE—Asian Games
83	Delhi, 1983:	First batch of Maruti car rolled out of the assembly line MEMORY CODE—Maruti Car
84	April 3, 1984:	Sq ldr Rakesh Sharma becomes India's first spaceman launched by the Soviet space aircraft Soyaz T-II MEMORY CODE Rakesh Sharma
85	Nov 6, 1985:	Garry Kasparov beat fellow Soviet player Anatoly Karpov to become the youngest ever world chess champion MEMORY CODE—Chess board
86	Jan 29, 1986:	American space satellite,

131

		Challenger, after successful launching, all the six on board killed. MEMORY CODE—6 killed passengers
87	June 8, 1987:	Swedish Govt. finds the Bofors paid commission to middle men for concluding arms purchase agreement with India. MEMORY CODE—Bofors Scam
88	Sept. 27, 1988:	Ben Johnson stripped off his 100 m gold medal for taking drugs; the medal awarded to Carl Lewis (US) MEMORY CODE—Drugs
89	Jan 20, 1989:	George Bush taken oath as the 41st President of US. MEMORY CODE—George Bush
90	Aug 7, 1990:	Govt. accepts Mandal Commission report providing for 27 per cent reservation for backward classes. MEMORY CODE—Mandal Commission
91	May 21, 1991:	Rajiv Gandhi killed in bomb blast MEMORY CODE—Rajiv Gandhi
92	June 4, 1992:	Harshad Mehta and others arrested MEMORY CODE—Share Scam
93	Nov 29, 1993:	JRD Tata passes away in Paris. MEMORY CODE—JRD Tata
94	Nov 2, 1994:	Sushmita Sen crowned Miss Universe. MEMORY CODE—Miss Universe
95	Jan 1, 1995:	World Trade Organization (WTO) comes into effect. European Union expands its membership to 15, the new ones being Austria, Finland

		and Sweden. MEMORY CODE—World Trade Organization.
96	May 17, 1996:	Vajpayee takes oath as Prime Minister and resigns on May 28, because BJP could not muster enough support. MEMORY CODE—Atal Bihari Vajpayee
97	Aug 31, 1997:	Princess of Wales Diana killed in a car accident. MEMORY CODE—Car Accident
98	Dec. 1, 1998:	Amartya Sen awarded Nobel Prize MEMORY CODE—Amartya Sen
99	Jan. 1, 1999:	European countries to have common currency: Euro, MEMORY CODE—Euro
100	Jan. 1, 2000:	Y2K problem MEMORY CODE—Y2K

You might have noted, at a few places, instead of selecting the personality as our memory image we selected the associated event as a memory code since the events give better scope of association than the name of the personality.

72

The Phonetics Method

In this method the numericals from 0-9 is given code e.g. 1 is called T or D.

First try to memorise the number codes with the help of hints provided which will give an aid for letter retention of the code.

No.	Code	Corresponding Hindi	Hint for memorizing
1.	t or d is one	ट या ड	The letter d or t has one down stroke
2.	n is 2	न	Letter n has two down strokes
3.	m is 3	म	Letter m has three down strokes
4.	r is 4	र	The last letter of four is r in many languages e.g. *char* (Hindi) *quitter* (Latin)
5.	L is 5	ल	Because in roman L is 50
6.	J (sh) (chg) (dg)	श, ज	J is mirror image of 6
7.	k is 7	क, ग	Two 7 make K (V and ^-K)
8.	f or v is 8	फ या व	Letter f is having 2 loops
9.	p or b is 9	प या ब	P/b have structure similar to 9
0.	S-O (Z)	स	

Once the memorization of the number code is complete with the help of hints provided, we can convert any number into a word or a word into number. This system will help us in memorizing reciprocals, square roots, cuberoots, cubes, tables etc.

Let's try to find words for the number from 13 to 15; we proceed in the following way:

13 consists of 1 and 3 that is t-m. inserting the first vowel 'a' we find the word *tam*.

14 consists of 1 and 4; that is t-r. inserting the 'a' we find *tar*.

15 consists of 1 and 5; that is t-1, inserting the 'a' & 'l' we find tail. Another possibility of 15 is *tall*, since the double L is translated by 5, not by 55. However, *tall* is an adjective and we cannot use it for associations.

If the insertion of the vowel 'a' does not lead to an appropriate word, we proceed to other vowels, always following the sequence of the alphabet.

For instance, 21 consists of 2 and 1, that is n-t. If we try to insert the first vowel 'a' we arrive at *nat*, which is not a meaningful word. Therefore we proceed to the next vowel, and find word '*net*' which is satisfactory.

22 equals n-n; we see that *nan, nen* and *nin* are not meaningful; the doubling of the fourth vowel, o, leads to the word '*Noon*' which is satisfactory.

Rule for Phonetics System

Pay attention only to the sound/pronunciation of the word and not the spelling.

For e.g.:-CAT: it does not consist of k but the sound is of *kat* so CAT will get converted into 71.

Similarly, *Case* (sounds like *kase*) so gets converted into 70 CUFF: 78

The word *cuff* does not convert into 788 but into 78. Since sound of 'f' appears only once.

Similarly TALL is 15 and not 155, BULL is 95 and not 955.

CHALK does not convert to 657 but into 67 since CHALK sounds as *Chak* (the L is silent).

In the same way PSYCHOLOGY gets converted into 0756 and not into 90756 since "p" is silent.

LODGE gets converted into 56 and not 516 since "D" is silent.
Let us try to convert some words into numbers:
MILK—357
TELEVISION—15802
MARUTI—341
Let's try to convert some bigger numbers into words:
224—NNR—NUNNERY
532—LMN—LAY MAN

6161—CHTCH—CHITCHAT

Here is the list of numbers from 1 to 100 with their substitute words in the same method. We need not memorise the list but it can be used as ready reference somewhere else in the book.

1. Tie	26. Niche	51. Lot	76. Cash
2. Hen	27. Neck	52. Lane	77. Cake
3. Ma	28. Navy	53. Lime	78. Cuff
4. Ray	29. Nap	54. Lair	79. Cap
5. Law	30. Mass	55. Lily	80. Face
6. Jaw	31. Mat	56. Lodge	81. Fat
7. Key	32. Man	57. Lake	82. Fan
8. Fee	33. Mama	58. Leaf	83. Fame
9. Bay	34. Mafia	59. Lap	84. Fare
10. Toes	35. Mail	60. Chase	85. Fall
11. Dad	36. Match	61. Chat	86. Fish
12. Den	37. Mike	62. Chain	87. Fig
13. Dam	38. Mafia	63. Chime	88. Five
14. Tar	39. Map	64. Chair	89. VIP
15. Tail	40. Nice	65. Chili	90. Base
16. Tissue	41. Rat	66. Judge	91. Bat
17. Deck	42. Rain	67. Cheque	92. Bean
18. Deaf	43. Ram	68. Chef	93. Beam
19. Tap	44. Rear	69. Chip	94. Bar
20. Nasa	45. Rail	70. Case	95. Ball
21. Net	46. Rash	71. Cat	96. Badge
22. Noon	47. Rake	72. Can	97. Back
23. Name	48. Rafia	73. Cam	98. Beef
24. Nero	49. Rope	74. Car	99. Bale
25. Nail	50. Lace	75. Coal	100. Thesis

73

The Personalized Meaning System

Now we are equipped with the memory language tools and memory ARROWS.

Let's use it in learning the ten foreign investors in India.

The top ten foreign investors in India (1992-June 1998) are the following:

Name of Countries	(Rs. Million)
1. USA	3,21,000
2. UK	82,000
3. Mauritius	64,000
4. South Korea	55,000
5. Japan	50,000
6. Germany	47,000
7. Israel	42,000
8. Cayman Island	36,000
9. Australia	31,000
10. Netherlands	29,000

Let's memorize it step by step:

Step 1: Identify the given data into LHS and RHS.

LHS	RHS
Name of Countries	(Rs. Million)
1. USA	3,21,000
2. UK	82,000
3. Mauritius	64,000
4. South Korea	55,000
5. Japan	50,000
6. Germany	47,000
7. Israel	42,000
8. Cayman Island	36,000
9. Australia	31,000
10. Netherlands	29,000

Step II: Convert the RHS using memory language.

Name of Countries	(Rs. Million)	Memory code
1. USA	3,21,000	—Mint
2. UK	82,000	—Asian Games
3. Mauritius	64,000	—Dog
4. South Korea	55,000	—Independence Day
5. Japan	50,000	—Ravan
6. Germany	47,000	—Rainbow
7. Israel	42,000	—Couple
8. Cayman Island	36,000	—Elephant's Trunk
9. Australia	31,000	—Legs
10. Netherlands	29,000	—Lollypop

Step III: In chapter 15 to 21 we have learned how to convert numericals into meaningful words.

Now we will learn how to give a better meaning to a word by Personalized Meaning System.

In this method we try to give a better meaning to a foreign word or relatively lesser known word, specially names.

In the present case let's try to give our own personalized meaning to the country names.

How To Form Personalized Meaning

The personalized meaning of word is based on the pronunciation of that particular word.

Let's understand it with the help of an example. In the present case let's try to give our own personalized meaning to the country's name.

10th Netherland: For most of us the word NETHERLANDS means just another country. Let's try to give a new meaning.

Try to observe the word NETHERLAND

Bifurcate the word to get a new meaning

NET—HER—LAND

We can give a new meaning by rearranging the words

NET—HER—LAND

HER—NET in Land

Now our new Meaningful picture for the word *Netherland* could be a lady (HER) with big (NET) covering a LAND.

Now both the LHS (Netherlands) and the RHS (29—lollypop) is having a new meaning/picture.

Step IV

Connect LHS to RHS through some picture

Our memory picture would be

Memory picture: Number of ladies (HER) trying to cover parts of LAND with number of NETS and the winner is given lollypop

(29) as a prize.
  For a moment concentrate on the mental image
  Try to see the mental image
  Clearly
  Colorfully
  In motion
  Similarly we shall learn the rest of the nine countries and their investment in India.
  9th

Australia	31000
Personalized meaning	**Memory code**
Ash Tray	Legs

Memory Image: See a picture of a person applying ash from a tray on his legs presuming it will improve his complexion.
  8th

Cayman Island	3600
Personalized meaning	**Memory code**
Key—man	Elephant pushing a log

Memory Image: Visualise a man with a big key and he is poking the elephant with the key to make the elephant push the log.
  7th

Israel	42000
Personalized meaning	**Memory code**
Israel	Couple

Memory Image: Is really the couple married? Neighbours murmured.
  6th

Germany	47000
Personalized meaning	**Memory code**
Many germs	Rainbow

Memory Image: Visualize many germs of seven colours forming a rainbow-like image.

5th

| Japan
Personalized meaning
Pan | 50000
Memory code
Ravan |

Memory Image: Visualize all the ten heads of the Ravan chewing pan.

4th

| South Korea
Personalized meaning
Seat Car | 55000
Memory code
Independence Day |

Memory Image: Chief guest of Independence Day celebration is made to sit on SEAT of CAR.

3rd

| Mauritius
Personalized meaning
Maur Shoes | 6400
Memory code
Dog |

Memory Image: Dog chasing a Mour (Peacock) with big shoes. Now two more countries UK and USA are left.

It is not necessary to find a substitute meaning for a word only by concentrating the pronunciation of the word.

Sometimes if we are already having some mental image about a particular word, we can use that image.

For example, the word UK might remind us of Diana

2nd

| UK
Personalized substitute
Diana | 82000
Memory code
Asian games |

Memory Image: Diana winning all the medals in Asian Games.

1st

| USA
Personalized substitute word
Bill Clinton | 321000
Memory code
Phonetic system
m-n-t
mint |

140

Memory Image: Bill Clinton bribing Monica by giving her mint so that she may withdraw case against him.

Here, we have seen how we can use PMS to memorize the list of countries with their investments.

In the coming chapter somewhere in the book we shall see how to use the PMS in learning:
1. Vocabulary
2. General Knowledge
3. Business GK
4. Names and faces

74

Indian Nobel Laureates

It is something we all remember. It is something which we all should not just remember but remember it precisely as they made us feel proud of our country because of their achievements.

We all know Rabindranath Tagore has got Nobel Prize for Literature but we are not very sure of the year in which he got it. Similarly we know C.V. Raman has got Nobel Prize for Physics but we are again not very sure of the year, nor are we sure of his study for which he got Nobel Prize.

It is true for most of us for other Nobel laureates.

Let us try to memorize the details using memory techniques.

Indian Nobel Laureates

Rabindranath Tagore (1861-1941): Author and educator. Founded Shantiniketan (1901) which later became Vishwabharati University. Tagore wrote love lyrics. *'Gitanjali'* and philosophical *'Sadhana'* are important works. He was awarded Noble Prize for Literature in 1913.

C.V. Raman (1888-1970): Physicist. Raman was born at Thiruvanikkaval near Tiruchirapalli in Tamil Nadu. Educated in Presidency College, Madras. Married to Lokasundari. Awarded Nobel Prize for Physics in 1930 for his study of the scattering of light. Popularly known as *'Raman Effect'*, the theory describes change in the frequency of light passing through transparent medium.

Hargobind Khorana (b. 1922): Now an American citizen, was born in Raipur, Punjab, now in Pakistan. He took his Ph. D. in chemistry from the University of Liverpool and in 1960 joined the University of Wisconsin. Khorana was awarded Nobel Prize for Medicine in 1968 for the interpretation of genetic code and its function in protein synthesis. He is married to a Swiss.

Mother Teresa (1910-1997): Was born to Alabanian parents in Skoplji, Yugoslavia and bapitized Agnes Gonxha Bojaxhin.

She came to India when she was 18 and took up teaching. She established a new congregation, *Missionaries of Charity*, which was approved by Vatican in 1950. Mother Teresa became an Indian citizen in 1948. She was awarded Nobel Prize for Peace in 1979.

Subramaniam Chandrasekhar (1910-1995): Born in Lahore (now in Pakistan), he was an American citizen. Educated in Presidency College, Madras. Nobel laureate C.V. Raman was his uncle. Married to Lalitha, who is also a physicist. Awarded Nobel Prize for Physics in 1983.

---

1. Rabindranath Tagore:
   Mental Picture: Visualise Rabindra Nath Tagore pouring coke (19-13) on his literary work to add value and flavour to it.
2. C.V. Raman: Since the face of C.V. Raman is not known to most of us, instead we can visualize Shri Raman holding his CV (Curriculum Vitae) in one hand and playing cricket (code for 30 is cricket) and the ball is the bulb causing lot of scattering of light.
3. Hargobind Khorana: Here also most of us are not familiar with his face. So to remember his name try to visualize Hairy Govinda (Har-Gobind) i.e., Govinda with hairs all around fall from horse (1968) and is treated with medicine. Further we can associate with his work (Interpretation of genetic code) by visualizing while getting treated the doctor is asking Hairy Govinda his genetic code.

Try the rest in a similar fashion.

75

How to Memorize Long Theory Having Data and Typical Names

Let's try to learn the scientific technique of memorizing a long theory consisting of data and typical names with the help of an example.

Let's try to memorize the passage given below using memory method.

History of National Flag

The design of the National Flag was made by an Andhra youth, Pingale Venkaiah. He presented a two-colour flag to Gandhiji for adoption as the Congress Party's flag. That was the time when the nationalists were agitating over the then prevailing flag which contained the Union Jack on the left hand top corner, symbolizing the Dominion status movement. This was not acceptable to most.

The emergence of Gandhiji on the scene and his visit to Bezwada in 1921 to attend the AICC meet marked the adoption of a new flag which Gandhiji accepted from young Venkaiah. The latter made his flag of two colours representing the two major communities in India alongwith a *charkha*, symbolizing progress. Venkaiah carried out the modifications on his advice. The *Tiranga* (Tricolor), thus, became virtually the flag of the national movement, although the official recognition came later.

The first national flag in India is said to have been hoisted on August 7, 1906 in the Parse Began Square (Green Park) in Calcutta. That flag was composed of horizontal stripes of red, yellow and green. The red stripe at the top had eight white lotuses embossed on it in a row. On the yellow stripe, the words *Vande Mataram* were inscribed in deep blue in Devanagri characters. The green stripe had a white sun on the left and a white crescent and a star on the right.

The second flag was hoisted in Paris by Madame Cama and her band of exiled revolutionaries in 1907 (according to some, in 1905). That was similar to the first flag except that the top stripe had only one lotus but seven stars denoting *Saptarishis*. The flag was also exhibited at a socialist conference in Berlin. By the time a third flag went up in 1917, our political struggle had taken a new turn. Annie Besant and Lokmanya Tilak hoisted it during the Home Rule Movement. This flag had five red and four green horizontal stripes arranged alternatively, with seven stars in the *Saptarishi* configuration superimposed on them. On the left hand top corner (the pole end) was the Union Jack. There was also a white crescent and a star in one corner.

The year 1931 was important in the history of the flag. A resolution was passed adopting Tricolor flag as our national flag. The flag was saffron, white and green: Saffron stood for courage and sacrifice; white for truth and peace; and green for faith and chivalry. It also carried a *charkha* in blue in the white band.

On July 22, 1947, Jawaharlal Nehru moved a resolution in the Constituant Assembly. It said, "Resolved that the National Flag of India shall be horizontal tricolor of deep saffron (*Kesari*), with white and dark green bands in equal proportions. In the centre of the white band there shall be a wheel in navy blue to represent the *chakra*. The design of the wheel shall be that of the wheel *chakra* which appears on the abacus of Ashoka's Sarnath Lion".

How to Memorize the Above Passage

Step I: Read first paragraph.

Step II: Quickly mark the key words in each of the sentences of the 1st paragraph.

The key words:
Pingale Venkaiah
Two-coloured flag.
Gandhiji
Union Jack
Dominion status movement.

Step III: Visualize the event and while visualizing give special attention to the key words, i.e., try to see the key words in exaggerated form i.e.,
1. Headed by Gandhi
2. Very big bright two-coloured glittering flag.

Step IV: (Important): Here we can easily realize that we are not able to visualize Pingale Venkaiah, Union Jack and Dominion status movement since we are not clear about its actual shape.

Here we can form a ridiculous picture by using personalized system; e.g., we can remember the name Pingale Venkaiah by visualizing a GIRL with PIN puncturing the VEN (kaiah) of the person who is coming to deliver a big flag to Gandhi.

Similarly, try some ridiculous associations for other key words.

Step V: Do the same for rest of the paragraphs. Wherever there is data, try to associate it with memory codes. For instance: The emergence of Gandhiji on the scene and his visit to Bezwada in 1921.

Memory Picture: Gandhiji trying to control Bada Baz (big eagle) with a stick (code for 21 is stick).

Step VI: Use overlearning principle as explained somewhere else in the book.

Step VII: Use spaced learning.

76

Mathematical and Scientific Data

In the previous chapters we have seen how the phonetics system can be used to memorise historical data. Now let's see applications of phonetics system in memorizing various important and difficult looking mathematical data.

1. π (pi) = 3.1416

Phonetics system conversion MDRDSH

Final meaningful word could be MaDRaDiSH

Remembering MaDRaDiSH as a value of π is much easier than to remember 3.1416 since MaDRaDiSH can be visualized.

e = 2.718281828

Final conversion could be

NeCk TouGH NaVy, TouGH NaVy.

2. There are numerous ways to develop mnemonic device to help you remember. How many professors or students you know, who can tell you how many zeros are there in a Quintillion? Here's a simple method to remember. There are 9 zeros in Billion. Think of subway Bill (Subway = 9 zeros)

12 zeros in a Trillion. Think of going to DeN is TRILL.

15 zeros in QUADRILLION. Think of a QUADLEGGED sTooL.

18 zeros in QUINTILLION. Think of a DeaF QUEEN.

21 zeros in SEXTILLION. Think of NeT Wearing girl looks sexy.

27 zeros in a OCTILLION. Think of sNaKe writhe like an OCTOPUS.

3. Let's see how phonetics system can be used to memorize the melting point of various elements.

(i) Iron melts at 1535°C. Tall MiL1

A blast furnace in a tall mill.

(ii) Lead melts at 327°C. MoNKey.

Picture yourself pouring lead into mold to make a lead monkey.

(iii) Silver melts at 1950°C. TaBLaS. Visualize Zakir Hussain playing a silver tabla.

DIAGRAMS

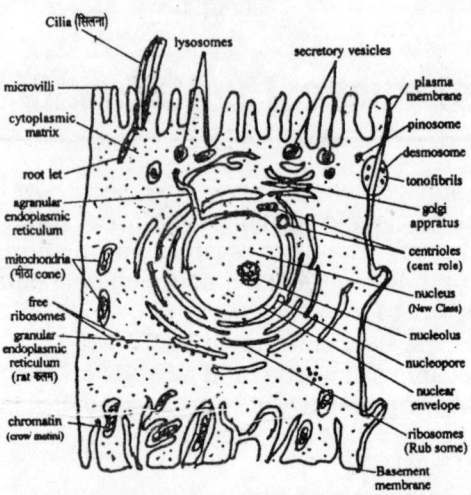

Cilia (सिलना)
lysosomes
secretory vesicles
plasma membrane
microvilli
cytoplasmic matrix
pinosome
desmosome
root let
tonofibrils
agranular endoplasmic reticulum
golgi appratus
mitochondria (पीठा cone)
centrioles (cent role)
nucleus (New Class)
free ribosomes
nucleolus
granular endoplasmic reticulum (rat कलम)
nucleopore
nuclear envelope
chromatin (crow maini)
ribosomes (Rub some)
Basement membrane

Ultrastructure of a typical animal cell as seen in the electron microscope.

Let me remind you of one crucial thing that all learning is done through association of the new thing to be learned to the thing which is already there in our memory. But in most of the learning we form association subconsciously (unknowingly).

Here, while memorizing we will attempt to learn the diagram by associating a known figure or a known picture to the new diagram to be learnt. Try to understand with an example.

To learn the above diagram we could follow the steps as given.

Step 1: Try to identify the diagram by looking at it from a different angle. i.e., try to think of a picture having similarity with the new diagram.

In the present e.g., the diagram can be compared with underocean view.

Step II: Associate different parts of the diagram with different parts of our own mental picture.

In the present diagram

1. Nucleus can be compared submarine in ocean.
2. Ribosomes can be compared with fishes surrounding the submarine.
3. Microvilli can be compared with sea waves.

4. Cilia can be compared with control tower for the submarine.

5. Membrane folds can be compared with plants under the ocean. Similarly, find associated picture for Golgi apparatus, Mitochondria etc.

Step III: Use PMS (Chapter—26) to associate the new word with the imaginary picture e.g.,

Using PMS we can convert nucleus into ® New Class and then associate it with submarine by thinking all the submarine crew are taking new class.

Ribosome: Ribbon—Some
Picture: Fishes
Association: Fishes are welcoming the submarine by flagging ribbon.

New word:	PMS
Microvilli:	microvillage

Picture: Sea waves
Association: All the microvillages are drowned in high sea waves

New word	PMS
Cilia	Chilli

Picture: Control tower
Association: The shape of control tower is similar to *chilli.*
Step IV: Follow Memory arrows.
Example 2:

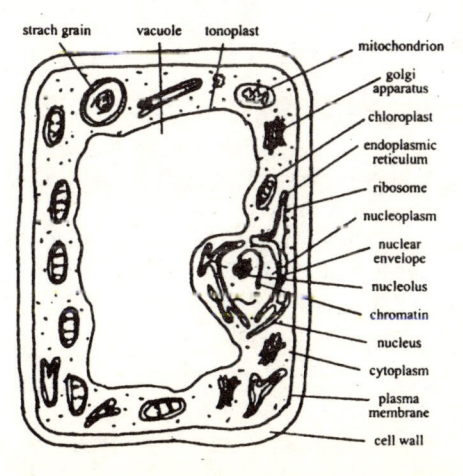

Ultrastructure of a typical plant cell as the electron microscope.

The immediate thing which may strike in our mind while looking at the diagram could be a mental picture of a big ground surrounded by walls (Cell Wall) at all the four sides with a swimming pool (Vacuole) and the swimming pool surrounded by tortoises (Chloroplast); the nucleus can be compared with a green room just outside the swimming pool.

As we have seen we can easily find a similar sound word for a new word so as to form an association. Similarly, with practice you will realize that for every diagram there could be an alternate known similar looking picture.

Tying the new diagram with known similar looking picture can make memorizing diagrams not just simple but also interesting.

RECIPROCALS

Here, we will memorize the reciprocals using phonetics method and memory code from 1 to 30.

Refer to the table and you will observe that every reciprocal is converted into word by using phonetics system.

Step I: Reciprocal of 28 is 0.0357. Here ignoring the zero since it appears in all the reciprocals after 10, we can convert 357 into milk.

357
MLK
Milk

Step II: The code for 28 is spectacles.

Step III: Associate the word spectacle with milk. We can do it simply by visualizing that we are inspecting milk for its purity by a spectacle.

Recalling process: Next time, whenever you need to recall reciprocal of 28, just recall the code for 28, i.e., spectacles and the word spectacles will remind you of the associated story of inspecting the milk.

And, hence, milk can simply be decoded to 357 and we can finally arrive at the reciprocal 0.0357.

Try to memorize rest of the reciprocals with the help of Memory Table provided:

Try to follow Memory Arrows:
Reciprocals

			Codes
1	1	1	SUN
2	0.5	2	SHOE
3	0.333	3	TREE
4	0.25	4	DOOR
5	0.2	5	WIFE
6	0.1666 WHITE CHALK	6	VICKS
7	0.1428 TEAR KNIFE	7	HEAVEN
8	0.125 TUNNEL	8	PLATE
9	0.111 DDT	9	WINE
10	0.1	10	HEN
11	0.0909 BUSYBEE	11	LEMON
12	0.0833 FOAMY MAMA	12	SHELF
13	0.0769 KEYSHOP	13	THRISTING
14	0.0714 EQUATOR	14	FORT IN
15	0.0666 CHO CHO SHOW	15	LIFT (ING)
16	0.0625 CHANNEL	16	SWEET SIXTEEN
17	0.0588 YELLOW LIFE	17	SETH IN
18	0.0555 LALA LALO	18	ATTACKING
19	0.0526 LUNCH	19	NUN THIN
20	0.05	20	AUNTY

Shape Method

21	0.0476 AIR COACH	21	STICK
22	0.0454 ROLLER	22	DUCK
23	0.0435 AIR MAIL	23	HEART
24	0.0417 RED KEY	24	CHAIR
25	0.04	25	HOOK
26	0.03851 AM FULL	26	HOCKEY STICK
27	0.037 MIKE	27	LAMP POST
28	0.0357 MILK	28	SPECTACLE
29	0.0345 MORAL	29	LOLLY POP
30	0.0333 MY MOM	30	BAT BALL

SQUARE ROOTS

Use the same technique for square roots.

Make sure you are having a gap of at least one week between the learning of square roots and reciprocals so as to avoid interference losses*. Use the same 30 memory codes as used for reciprocals.

Square Roots

No.	Sq. roots	Codes
10	3.162	Touch in
11	3.317	Mattock
12	3.464	Archer
13	3.605	Chisel
14	3.741	Carrot
15	3.873	Vaccum
16	4	
17	4.123	Denim
18	4.24	Nari
19	4.359	My lip
20	4.472	Organ
21	4.58	Leaf
22	4.69	Gypsy
23	4.796	Cabbage
24	4.90	Bus
25	5	
26	5.099	Baby
27	5.196	Two Page
28	5.291	Naptha
29	5.385	Muffle
30	5.477	Rawcake

***Interference losses:** When material of similar nature are attempted to learn together or when the gap between the learning of one set of material and other set of SIMILAR materials is less, the similarity may cause some confusion resulting in memory losses called interference losses.

CUBE ROOTS

Referring the table for cube roots from 1 to 30 it is clear that before 8 all the cube roots have 1 at the unit place. From 8 to 20 all the cube roots have 2 in the unit place and 27 to 30 all the cube roots have 3 in their unit place.

So, while memorizing cube roots using memory code and phonetics method we will ignore the unit digit.

In the table alternate word for the digits after decimal are given. Here, we will use the code numbers from 1 to 30. Since we have already used these memory codes twice instead we will use memory codes from 31 to 60 i.e. the memory code 31 will represent 1 and 60 will represent 30. Use Memory Arrows

Codes For Cube Roots

Nos.	Root	Code
2	1.26	NACH
3	1.44	ROWER
4	1.57	LAUGHING
5	1.71	GODDESS
6	1.817	VODKA
7	1.91	PODIUM, BOTTOM
8	2	
9	2.08	SAFI
10	2.15	TAILOR
11	2.22	NUNNERY
12	2.29	KNOB, NIPPO
13	2.35	MALLET
14	2.42	RADIUM
15	2.47	ROCK
16	2.52	LION
17	2.57	LOCKET
18	2.62	CHAINS
19	2.67	CHEEK
20	2.71	GUTTOR
21	2.75	CLUB
22	2.80	HIVES
23	2.84	FARRARI
24	2.88	FIFER
25	2.92	BANNER
26	2.962	PIGEON
27	3	
28	3.03	SMOOCH
29	3.072	SKIN
30	3.107	DESK

CUBES

Use the same method to memorize cubes. For your reference a cube table with alternate words are given.

Nos.	cubes	codes	Nos.	cubes	codes
6	216		19	6859	shuffle bee
7	343		20	8000	
8	512		21	9261	punched
9	729		22	10648	toss giraffe
10	1000		23	12167	tent jack

Nos.	cubes	codes	Nos.	cubes	codes
11	1331		24	13824	hot movie nara
12	1728	toffee knife	25	15625	
13	2197	no tobacco	26	17576	dog loggage
14	2744	Hungary hero	27	19683	white page fame
15	3375				
16	4096	race beach	28	21952	wind up lion
17	4913	rub tummy	29	24389	neero move up
18	5832	Leo heavy women	30	27000	

Few places are left blank deliberately for you to attempt.

FORMULAE

Throughout my school I found the formulae to be the most difficult thing to be memorized. In the previous chapters we have seen a number of mnemonic techniques to memorize various things like historical data, passages, vitamins, periodic tables, vocabulary etc. Unfortunately those techniques will not help us in memorizing formulae but there is certainly something we can do to memorize formulae efficiently.

Let's try to understand how to attempt in the best way to memorize formulae in steps.

Step 1: Generate a formulae note book. Cultivate a habit of accumulating formulae and maintaining it in a single place. Remember we can memorise a particular material more perfectly if we are revising it from a SINGLE place and prefarably written in our own HANDWRITING.

Step II: Sometimes while recalling the formulae in exams we confuse by thinking whether it is plus or minus or whether it is Cos q or Sin q or whether it is Tan q or tan q/2. Try to identify the symbols which may confuse you or which confuses you more often. Then mark those symbols with red pen in your formulae book.

Those symbols will stand out every time you revise and will attract an extra attention which is needed. Red is having the longest wavelength so it stands out more in comparison to the other colour. It is because of this reason red is used in ambulance lights etc.

Step III: Revise the formulae more often; formulae requires number of revision with frequency 3:1, if we compare with the other syllabus content (like passages etc) since formulae is abstract and we cannot visualize it.

Step IV: Try to utilize the principles of Memory Arrows wherever possible.

CHEMISTRY

We can memorize the positions of various elements in the periodic table by simple rule of acronym.

Let's try to learn period II of the periodic table.

Elements of the IInd period of the periodic table.

	Element	Symbol	Atomic No.
1.	Lithium	Li	3
2.	Berylium	Be	4
3.	Boron	B	5
4.	Carbon	C	6
5.	Nitrogen	N	7
6.	Oxygen	O	8
7.	Flourine	F	9
8.	Neon	Ne	10

Let us try to form a sentence containing all the symbols in the same order.

Lilly   Berry   Born   Capricorn

Naturally Studied at Oxford than at Flora Nagar.

Now the initial alphabets of the words will give the clue of the elements and also we can get the atomic number from the sentence since all the sequence of elements is maintained in it.

Period III of the periodic table.

S.No.	Element	Symbol	Atomic No.
1	Sodium	Na	11
2	Magnesium	Mg	12
3	Aluminum	Al	13
4	Silicon	Si	14
5	Phosphorus	P	15
6	Sulphur	S	16
7	Chlorine	Cl	17
8	Argon	Ar	18

Memory sentence for period III

Soda (Na) from Mango tree (Mg) eliminates (Al) silky (Si) and fussy (P) sulphar (s) and clears (Cl) arguments (Ar)

Since the period IV is quite lengthy (18 elements) so it would be simpler to divide the period in 2 or 3 parts and make two or three sentences for each.

For instance for first five elements of period IV, i.e., period V:

S.No.	Element	Symbol	Atomic No.
1	Potassium	K	19
2	Calcium	Ca	20
3	Scandium	Sc	21
4	Titanium	Ti	22
5	Vanadium	V	23

Memory sentence could be

Potato (K) from Calcutta (Ca) are sent (Si) by Trucks (Ti) and Vans (V).

Similarly try to form memory sentence for other elements.

BIOLOGY

I have seen in my career as a memory teacher that students often confuse when it comes to various vitamins, its scientific names, its chief metabolic functions and effect of deficiency.

Vitamins, their year of discovery, chief metabolic functions and effects of deficiency:

Fat-soluble vitamins

Vitamin A (Retinol)—1913:
Essential for normal growth and development, for normal function of epithelia cells and normal development of teeth and bones. Prevents night blindness.

Retarded growth. Reduced resistance to infection.

Abnormal function of gastrointestinal, genitourinary, and respiratory tracts due to altered epithelia membranes. Interferes with production of 'night purple'.

Vitamin D

(Cholecalciferol)—1925:
Regulates absorption of calcium and phosphorus from the intestinal tract. Affords antiricketic activity.

Interferes with utilization of calcium and phosphorus in bone and teeth formation. Development of bone disease, rickets, caries.

Vitamin E

(Tocopherols)—1936: Protects tissues, cell membranes, and

Vitamin A against peroxidation. Helps strengthen red blood cells.
Decreased red blood cell resistance to rupture.

Vitamin K

(Phytomenadione)—1935
Essential for formation of normal amounts of prothrombin for blood coagulation.
Diminished blood clotting time. Increased incidence of heamorrhages.

Water-soluble Vitamins

Vitamin B1 (Thiamin)—1936: An important aid in carbohydrate metabolism. Needed for proper functioning of the digestive tract and nervous system. Beriberi, loss of muscle, loss of appetite, impaired digestion of starches & sugars. Various nervous disorders, coordination.

Vitamin B2

(Riboflavin) 1935: Needed in formation of certain enzymes and in cellular oxidation. Prevents inflammation of oral mucous membranes and the tongue. Impaired growth, lassitude and weakness. Causes cheillosis or glossittis. May result in photophobia and cataracts.

Vitamin B6

(Pyridoxine) 1934: Acts, as do other B vitamins, to break down protein, carbohydrate and fat. Acts as a catalyst in the formation of niacin from tryptophan.
Increased irritability, convulsions, and peripheral neuritis. Anorexia, nausea & vomiting.

Vitamin B12

(Cyanocobalamin) 1948: Essential for development of red blood cells. Required for maintenance of skin, nerve tissue, bone and muscles.
Results in pernicious anaemia. Weakness, fatigue, sore and cracked lips.

Vitamin C

(Ascorbic Acid) 1919: Needed to form the cementing substance, collagen, in various tissues (skin, dentine, cartilage, and bone matrix). Assists in wound healing, bone fractures;

lower resistance to infections, susceptibility to dental cavities, pyorrhoea, & bleeding gums. Delayed wound healing. Specific treatment for scurvy.

In this chapter we will see that how our memory technique can help us in remembering all these.

Now read the first Vitamin; i.e., Vitamin A, its scientific name its function and effect of deficiency.

Mental Picture:

Vitamin A—Retinol
Visualize Apple (code for A)
Visualize a Rat is pushing an Apple inside a Tap and in the process its skin got stuck with a nearby nail and only the skeleton of the rat is left. Further we can visualize that the Rat is unable to locate the nail on which his skin was stuck since he is having night blindness problem.

Vitamin B1 (thiamin)

B—Mental code is bag
1—Mental code is sun
Thiamin—Thumb in
Mental image: Visualize you are trying to put SUN with thumb in the BAG. In the process your thumb got burnt. Not just your thumb but also your tongue (loss of appetite) and also your digestive system got burnt. Was a very very (Beri Beri) simmering sensation.

The above mental picture can help us in recalling all the important metabolic functions and deficiencies and also the scientific name of Vitamin B1. More importantly with these mental picture the problem of getting confused with the functions and deficiencies with the other can be eliminated.

In case we are interested in memorizing the year of discovery of various vitamins we can just associate the year code with vitamin code e.g.:

Vitamin A

Year of discovery: 1913
Code for A—Apple
Code for 13—coke tin.
Mental Picture: Visualize apple inside the coke's tin instead of the drink.

Similarly try to memorize the details of other vitamins with the memory techniques.

77

Generally Knowledge Often Confuses Us

ISO stands for International Organisation for Standardization and has its head office at Geneva, Switzerland. It comprises National standard bodies of 91 countries including India. ISO, 9000 was developed in 1987.

ISO 9000 series has 5 standards, viz., ISO 9000, ISO 9001, ISO 9002, ISO 9003, and ISO 9004.

ISO 9000: Provides guidelines for selection and use of a series of ISO 9001, ISO 9002, ISO 9003, and ISO 9004. This standard is, therefore, not to be used for contractual purpose.

ISO 9001: Model for Quality Assurance in design, development, production, installation and servicing. This is for use when the contract specially requires that the supplier assures quality throughout the whole cycle from design through production, installation and servicing.

ISO 9002: Model of quality assurance in production, installation and servicing. This is for use when the specified requirements for products are stated in terms of an already established design or specification.

ISO 9003: Model of quality assurance in final inspection and testing. This is applicable where only the supplier's capabilities for inspection and tests can be satisfactorily demonstrated.

ISO 9004: Quality management and quality system elements. This is for internal use which describes a basic set of quality system elements which help to develop a sound and comprehensive quality management system.

Once we memorize the above and after a period of time when we need to recollect we may get confused. We may think for inspection and test whether it is ISO 9002 or ISO 9003 Or

ISO 9001 is for assurance in design, development, production, installation and servicing or just for assurance in production, installation and servicing.

Here we can use the Phonetic system to lock permanently the particular ISO with their titles.

Example: For ISO 9001 and ISO 9002 the confusion part is DESIGN which is with 9001 and not with 9002.

Memory Image: Just visualize you are making a complicated design with paint and brush on your Tie (1 of 9001)

ISO 9003

Mental Image: You are surprised to see your Ma (3 of 9003) coming to your school for INSPECTION and TEST.

ISO 9004: It is about quality management but since QUALITY is an abstract word so we will imagine Quality Ice-cream for QUALITY.

Mental Image: Checking the Internal quality of Quality Ice-cream with X-Ray (4 of 9004)

Companies		Turnover (Rs. Crore) 97-98
1.	Hindustan Lever	8528
2.	Reliance Industries	13759
3.	Telco	7450
4.	Bajaj Auto	3447
5.	Larsen & Tubro	5841
6.	ICICI	5964
7.	Gujarat Ambuja Cement	952
8.	Wipro	1442
9.	Nestle India	1434
10.	NIIT	333

To memorize Bajaj Auto having turnover of Rs. 3447 Crores, just group the figure as 34 47 and use the standard code.

Mental Image: A MaRe riding Bajaj scooter rammed it on a gigantic RacK placed on the road.

	Turnover
Telco	Rs. 7450 Crores
	CaR LaCe

Mental Image: Telco's latest car, Indica car with an additional safety feature i.e., CaR fitted with LaCe which can be tied to a nearby lamp post to avoid any theft.

	Turnover
Gujarat Ambuja Cement	Rs. 952 Crores
	P L N
	PLaNe.

Mental Image: Imagine a gigantic aero PLaNe made up of Cement.

Remembering Various Acts, Sections, Subsections, Clauses and Subclauses

This section is specially for the students of law, CA and CS where we have to remember around 60 to 70 acts and each act may consist of some 20 to 650 sections. Again each section may consist of a dozen or two subsections which involve a number of clauses and then subclauses. The huge volume and the abstract numbering of sections create a lot of confusion. Here is a scientific way to lock various sections permanently.

Let's try to understand with an example:

The Indian Contract Act

Section 14: "Free consent" defined
Section 17: "Fraud" defined
Section 58: Alternative promise, one branch illegal.

Now we know through Phonetics Method 14 is DooR, 17 is DecK and 58 is LeaF.

Section 14
Mental Image: You have kept your DooR open and given CONSENT that anybody can FREELY enter your home.

Section 17
Mental Image: You bought a DecK and ultimately found that it was just a FRAUD as you were given only the outer covering of DecK, empty from inside.

Section 58
Mental Image: Visualize the Lea Ves on one of the BRANCH is artificial and hence ILLEGAL.

Similarly we can remember other sections using phonetics methods.

Still two questions are unanswered.

Q1. We have around 65 Acts and in each Act Section 14 is different. Will we not confuse as now we have to associate DooR (14) 65 times, once with each act?

Q2. In the chapter, 'The Phonetics Method' we have just 100 memory codes. However, the number of section in each law is much more than that. How to deal with sections beyond 100?

Ans 1. Yes, we have to associate DooR (14) 65 times and our natural memory will take care and help us in avoiding confusion.

Remember

"We confuse or forget only when we are worried about confusion or forgetting."

Ans 2. To deal with section beyond 100 we can create our own code.

For instance, for section 101

101

D S D/T

D u S T

Or for 121—DeNt

For your convenience I am providing you with a few more memory codes:

101—DusT
102—De SigN
103—Di S May
104—De Se Rt
105—Die SeL
106—Do Sa Ge
107—DeSK
108—aDhe Sive
109—ToSS uP
110—iDioTS
111—DDT
112—TiTaN
113—DiaDeM—A crown
114—Daugh TeR
115—TiTLe
116—Ho TdiSH
117—TooTh—aCHe
118—TeeD—oFf
119—DeaTH Bed
120—Te NniS
121—Te NT
122—WhiTe—NuN
123—DeNiM
124—DiNer
125—TuNneL
126—DaNiSH—A native of Denmark
127—DoNKey
128—Wet NaVy
129—DeMiSe
130—ADMiT
131—DeMaND
132—whiTe MeN
133—ToMoRRow
134—hoT MeaL

135—DaMaGe
136—aToMic
137—hoT MoVie
138—DuMP
139—DreSS
140—DiRT
141—DRaiN
142—DRuM
143—DRyeR
144—DriLL
145—ToRcH
146—DRaG
147—TRoPhy
148—TRooP
149—DiALS
150—ToiLeT
151—Two Line
152—DiLeMma
153—DoLlar
154—DealeR
155—DeLiLah : False woman
156—DeLuGe : A great flood
157—TaLe
158—Tea LeaF
159—TuLiP
160—auDaCiouS
161—DiGiT
162—DuDGeoN : State of strong anger
163—TeaCh Me
164—DiTcher
165—hot JuLy
166—aDJudGe
167—hoT JuG
168—heaD ChcF
169—Tea ShoP
170—DecKS
171—TicKeT
172—ToKeN
173—OuTCoMe
174—TiGeR
175—TicKLe
176—DoG WaTcH
177—DiGgiNG

178—TaKe Off
179—whiTe CaP
180—DoVeS
181—DaViD
182—DiVaN
183—DeFaMe
184—DiVeR
185—DeViL
186—TouGH Jaw
187—whiTe WiG
188—hoT FiFe
189—TouGH Boy
190—ToPaZ
191—DePuTy
192—Thigh BoNe
193—whiTe BeaM
194—DiPpeR
195—TaBLe
196—whiTe PaGe
197—ToBaCco
198—TiP oFf
199—whiTe PuPpy
200—NoSeS
201—NeST

I have mastered 1000 codes and they are in use routinely. I have not listed them here beyond 201. This is deliberate, so you might be encouraged to develop the habit of composing your own words. By all means, do this. It's fun.

Historical Data

We can use our memory system to memorise historical data. The method is similar to the method used in "Top ten investors".

1921—Gandhiji assumed leadership of the Congress Party. We know that the code for 21 is stick.

Mental Picture: Gandhiji is controlling his followers with a big stick.

1933—Hitler became Chancellor of Germany.
Code for 33 is bow.

Mental Picture: Hitler is aiming at a big chancellor cigarette with a bow.

1927—Television demonstrated for the first time.
Code for 27—Lamp Post

Mental Picture: A big crowd is watching TV under a lamp post.

Here in all the three cases we have not included the century year i.e., 19 since we know that we will not confuse them with any other century.

Use the memory system to memorise other historical events as given:

Glimpses of World History

A.D.
1869	— Suez Canal opened for traffic.
1870	— Unification of Germany by Bismark.
1895	— Roentgen discovered X-rays.
1896	— Marconi invented wireless.
1899	— Beginning of the Boer War.
1904	— Outbreak of Russo-Japanese War.
1905	— Battle of Sea of Japan: Japan defeated Russia. Einstein discovered the Theory of Relativity.
1911	— Chinese Revolution.
1912	— Establishment of Chinese Republic
1914	— Outbreak of World War 1: Panama Canal opened.
1917	— Russian Revolution began on March 8 and culminated successfully in October.
1918	— World War I ended on November 11.
1919	— Treaty of Versailles signed.
1920	— League of Nations was founded.
1921	— Gandhiji assumed leadership of Congress Party.
1922	— Mussolini marched on to Rome.
1923	— Hitler wrote *Mien Kampf* in jail.
1927	— Television demonstrated for the first time.
1931	— Japan began occupation of Manchuria.
1933	Hitler became Chancellor of Germany.
1935	— Hitler defied Versailles Treaty and re-established universal military training in Germany.
1936	— Spanish Civil War began; abdication of Edward VIII.
1938	— Chamberlain signed the Munich Pact with Hitler with pious hopes of peace in our time.

1939	World War II began on September 1.
1940	Germans entered the undefended city of Paris.
1941	Japanese attack of Pearl Harbour.
1943	Casablanca Conference.
1945	Yalta Agreement was signed by Roosevelt, Churchill and Stalin; U.N.O. founded; atom bomb dropped on Hiroshima and Nagasaki; End of Second World War.
1946	First meeting of UN Assembly opened in London on January 10.
1947	Partition of India; India got her Independence on August 15.
1948	Independence of Burma and Sri Lanka; Communists came to power in China.
1951	Japanese Peace Treaty signed.
1952	Queen Elizabeth II came to the throne of England.
1953	Death of Stalin; Conquest of Mt. Everest.
1955	Bandung Conference.
1956	Nationalization of Suez Canal.
1957	Russia launched first artificial earth satellite Sputnik 1.
1958	Ayub Khan became military dictator of Pakistan.
1959	Russia launched a Sputnik round the earth on 2nd January.
1960	Election of John F. Kennedy as President of U.S.A.
1961	Man's first entry into outer space.
1962	Algeria freed; Chinese aggression against India.
1963	Partial Nuclear Test Ban Treaty signed by the Big Three; Russia sent Woman cosmonaut Valentine Tereshikova into outer space; John F. Kennedy, President of USA, ASSASSINATED; Federation of Malaysia came into being; Kenya and Zanzibar became free.

Business G.K.

Let's apply our memory techniques to learn table-I and table II. Here we will apply our memory code + personalized meaning system.

Example
Name	CEO	Turnover (crore)
Essar Steel	Shashi Ruia	2500

Memory Steps

Essar—Personalized meaning—Ass are
Shashi Ruia—Personalized memory picture—Shashi Kapoor
Memory Code for 25 is Hook
Memory Picture—Picture that Shashi Kapoor is sitting on Ass and controlling it with a big hook.

Here our aim is not just to learn the memory codes but to learn it so perfectly that you are able to recall all the codes very spontaneously and promptly.

Your effectiveness in learning through memory language is directly proportionate to your mastering of the 100 memory codes.

For your convenience a chart of 100 codes with pictures is provided which could be pasted on the study table.

COMPANIES, CEOs AND TURNOVER

Sl. No.	Name	CEO	Turnover (Rs. Crore)	Products
1.	TELCO	Ratan Tata	35000	Light/Medium/Heavy Vehicles, Passenger Cars, Spare Parts and Excavators
2.	Reliance	Dhirubhai Ambani	13404	Textiles, Petroleum Industries, Petrochemicals, Power
3.	Grasim Industries	Kumar Mangalam Birla	2000	Iron, Cement, Textile, Paper
4.	Mahindra & Mahindra	Keshub Mahindra		Jeep and Tractors
5.	Bajaj Auto	Rahul Bajaj	3100	Scooters, Motor Cycles, Auto
6.	HLL	Kekib Dadiseth	8343	Soaps, Synthetic Detergents, Hydro Gena Oil, Vanaspati, Personal Products, Fine Chemicals, Packaged Tea, Xice Cream etc.
7.	L & T Ltd	S D Kulkarni		Cement, Switch Gear, Industrial Machinary, Chemical Plant & Machinary

#	Company	Person	Amount	Business
8.	ITC Ltd	YC Deveshwar	526.20 (Net Profit)	Cigarettes, Printed Materials, Marine Products, Hotel
9.	Essar Steel	Shashi Ruia	2500	Shipping, Marine, Telecom, Oil Exploration, Cellphone
10.	Escorts	Rajan Nanda	3400	Agri Machinary, Two Wheelers
11.	Indo Rama	Om Prakash Lohia	1453	Textiles, Synthetics
12.	Ranbaxy	Dr Parminder Singh	1323	Pharmaceuticals
13.	Arvind Mills	Arvind Narottam Lalbhai	1000	Largest Denim Suppliers, Dyes
14.	Videcon	Venugopal N Dhoot		TV, Stereo Consumer International Durables etc.
15.	Tata Exports	Syamal Gupta	1706	Automobiles, Steels, Leather Products
16.	Indian Rayon	Kr. Mangalam Birla	1817	Filament Yarn, Hose, Grey Cement, Pipe
17.	Ballarpur	Lalit Mohan Thaper		Newsprintpaper, Chemicals Industries, Agro Business
18.	Ispat Industries	M L Mittel	1454	Steel Sheets, Galvenised Coil, Steel Products
19.	Wipro	Azim H Premji	1830	Service Technology, Consumer Products.
20.	BPL	Ajit G. Nambiar		Consumer Electronics, T.V., Stereo etc.
21.	Appollo Tyres	Onkar Singh Kanwar	1300	Tyres

78

Remember Every Appointment

From my own experience, I am pretty sure that once in a while you must have happened to forget an appointment or something that you intended to do during the day or during the week. Perhaps that was one of the reasons why you took up memory training. And I am equally sure that it will not happen again if you follow the rules laid down in this chapter.

As far as the current day is concerned, there is no difficulty in applying my system since the basic list (in phonetics method chapter) provides everything we need. If you have to see your hairdresser at 9 A.M., all you have to do is to associate him with Bee and picture that he is placing bee-hives on your head, since that is the latest hair style. Or if you have to remember that you must ring your boss at 7 A.M. just visualize your boss holding a Key (code for 7) of your promotion and growth.

However, our task becomes somewhat more difficult when it comes to remembering appointment of the whole week rather than for one day. A plan of work for a single day can be kept in mind by an average person without using any memory system. But when the question of remembering weekly timetable crops up, specially if the appointments and assignments vary from day to day, the persons with untrained memory have two alternatives: either he forgets the half do and as a result suffers on disputes or he jots down each item in his appointment book. By doing so it is true that he manages to keep a close track of his appointments, yet he is thereby damaging his memory, for as we know by this time, reliance upon putting everything down in black and white has a decidedly harmful effect upon systematic memory training.

Now how can we apply our system to a time table that comprises activities for an entire week? By this time we had enough experience to know that we must link up this problem in some way or the other with our basic series of key words.

In order to achieve a reduction of this sort, number the days of the week as follows:

Sunday	—	1
Monday	—	2
Tuesday	—	3
Wednesday	—	4
Thursday	—	5
Friday	—	6
Saturday	—	7

After we have identified the days of the week with numbers 1 to 7 in this fashion, we add to them the particular hours of the day which are to be remembered. Here are some examples:

Since Sunday is 1 we think 2 o'clock on Sunday as 12
4 o'clock on Sunday as 14
7 o'clock on Sunday as 17, etc.
So we arrive at
8 o'clock of Monday as 28   — *Navy*
9 o'clock of Saturday as 77   — *Cake*
5 o'clock of Thursday as 55   — *LiLly*

Then the association with the assignment which you are to undertake is made in the accustomed manner.

Below I list as an example 6 appointments which you have made for a week, and in the listing I purposely do not follow any chronological order. This is because in everyday life we do not, of course, make an appointment, first for a Sunday, then for Monday, next for Tuesday, etc., rather we must accept and memorize the appointments as they occur and still be able to recall them in chronological order so that no appointment is overlooked.

Here is how the method works. Suppose you have an appointment with your insurance broker on Monday at 5 P.M. Monday at 5 P.M. is translated into 25 or Nail. The association between Nail and insurance broker is not difficult if we just visualize that you are making a claim for your broken Nail from your insurance broker.

In this manner we arrive at the following associations for remembering these appointments.

Monday at 5: Appointment with insurance broker.
Wednesday at 1 : Playing cricket
Mental Image : Playing Cricket with RaT (41)
Saturday at 6 : Meeting the school principal
Mental Image : Giving the principal a CaSH (76) as fees.
Tuesday at 2 : Lunch with a friend.

Mental Image : Having lunch in MooN (32)
Thursday at 8 : Going for Shopping
Mental Image : Shopping and putting things into bag made of LeaVes (58)
Sunday at 2 : Going for movie
Mental Image : Going to the DeN to (12) watch a movie.

Telephone Numbers

One of the most frequent applications of Phonetic system is remembering Telephone Numbers. We need Telephone Numbers constantly, and it is rather annoying and time wasting to look them up every time we want to ring somebody.

Let's start with my own mobile number—9811139474.

If you are a resident of Delhi then you know, for Essar mobile the first 5 digits are 98111. So we ignore the first 5 digits since our natural memory can well take care of it and for 39474 m b r k r

By concentrating for just 3-4 seconds we can arrive at some meaningful words, out of this 5 letters i.e., My BroKeR, and finally just associate the phrase, My BroKeR with me.

One of the associations could be My BroKeR is Biswaroop's best friend.

Or

Biswaroop is My BroKeR in land selling deal.

Another Example

Phone Number of Diamond Pocket Books is 684 1033 (New Delhi).

Most of the time we are able to recollect the first digits of the telephone numbers, since we know (if we are residing in Delhi), for South Delhi the telephone number starts with 6 and for Daryaganj side it starts with 3 etc.

So we will ignore the first digit and concentrate on the rest
                    684 1033
                    f R T S m m

Little brainstorming helps us in getting
FoRTS Ma Ma

Mental Image: Chacha Chaudhuri (Famous Character of Diamond Comics) going to various FoRTS in search of his MaMa.

Another example

The Times of India: 3312277 (again ignore the first digit-3)

M T M N K K

Alternate word: Ma Ti Nee No Cake

Mental Image: Today *The Times of India* has published a news that in MaTiNee show No Cake will be available in the Moviehall canteen.

My ten most important telephone numbers

1. ....
2. ....
3. ....
4. ....
5. ....
6. ....
7. ....
8. ....
9. ....
10. ....

79

Total Recall

Find out how much you have absorbed. This book can help you in remembering everything ELSE if you remember the contents of this book.

With the help of the keywords, try to write the gist of that particular chapter in the blanks. Don't hesitate to refer to the chapter if you are unable to make out the chapter from the clue.

	Keywords	Gist of Chapters
1.	Involve yourself	_____
2.	Combination of subjects	_____
3.	24 hours / 7 days	_____
4.	45 minutes / 10 minutes	_____
5.	Auto-suggestion	_____
6.	Conscious association	_____
7.	Visualization	_____
8.	1st letter word	_____
9.	Revisiting	_____
10.	1/3 of total time	_____
11.	Spider notes	_____
12.	Incomplete task	_____
13.	Mental rehearsal	_____
14.	Estimation	_____
15.	Word number	_____
16.	Clock exercise	_____
17.	Number series	_____
18.	See, smell, taste, feel	_____
19.	Enjoyment	_____
20.	Break boundaries	_____
21.	Attention	_____
22.	Think opposite	_____
23.	Physical exercise	_____
24.	Present-mindedness	_____

25. Link confusion   _____
26. Clue method   _____
27. Representative word   _____
28. Phonetic method   _____
29. Bits   _____
30. Water   _____
31. Morning meal   _____
32. Apple   _____
33. Sketch   _____
34. Verbalization   _____
35. Peak alertness time   _____
36. Debate   _____
37. Reminders   _____
38. Puzzle   _____
39. Major events   _____
40. Caffeine   _____
41. Snacks   _____
42. *Pranayam*   _____
43. Permanent storage place   _____
44. Mental Notes   _____
45. Left hand   _____
46. New place   _____
47. Out of routine   _____
48. Smell memory   _____
49. Number association   _____
50. Mind power   _____
51. Stop worrying   _____
52. Dummy pill effect   _____
53. Checklist   _____

Animal	Body wt. (Kilogram)	Brain wt. (gram)
Elephant	800	6000
Whale	1500	5000
Lion	180	300
Monkey	60	100
Bat	0.1	3
Human being	60	1450

80

Common Memory Failures and Their Solutions

Hand Brake

Q. 1. I was suffering from migraine and was in great deal of pain. I myself drove my car to my family doctor. On the way back home, I parked the car and instantly went inside my home and started speaking to my sister unware of the fact that I had forgotten to put the hand brake on. When my sister reminded me, I rushed back towards the car but to my surprise my neighbour had put the hand brake on.

Ravi, Patna

Answer: Pain often causes distraction and leads to memory lapse. In such a condition we pay extra attention to medication and often avoid driving, etc. and even if you cannot avoid driving yourself be extra careful to check your car when you park it.

Reaching Early

Q. 2. Once I along with my wife, brother and my sister-in-law decided to have a holiday in Jaipur. Accordingly, we booked our tickets and my wife kept them in a safe place. On the appointed day, we reached the hotel where we had made an advance booking and the clerk told us that we were a day earlier. All our holidaying was spoilt. For a few minutes, we started blaming one another. It was only later we realized that my wife had arranged the booking and she had forgotten the exact date.

Anand, Meerut

Answer: Sometimes, over-confidence and too much dependence takes us to such a situation. Prior to your visits, each of you should have the exact information. You relied heavily on your wife, that too was mistaken.

In any situation when more than two people are involved, it is imperative that each one should share responsibility. You should have the habit of checking everything whenever you plan an outing. In such cases, making a timetable will make your trip balanced and enjoyable.

Instant Reply

Q. 3. As a PRO, I have to deal with people from different walks of life. On one such occasion, I had to interview a designer for the required post in my organisation. I asked him about his last important assignment. After the interview finished cordially, in a jovial mood, he repeated the same question to me. To my surprise, I could not reply instantly and escaped the question. But I am still feeling frustrated over my failure to recollect that query.

Mahinder, Madras

Answer: It is a paradox that even a professional, who is appreciated for his devotion to his job, fails to get retrieval of his personal information. This "absent-minded" situation puts him in an awkward situation. It is well known that anxiety often causes memory loss. The best is to relax as much as you can. Of course your single-minded devotion on what you are doing is important. With more preparation and confidence, you can easily stave off anxiety and then reallocate your attention.

Forgetting Shoes

Q.4. Ten years ago, I bought a new costly pair of shoes. At the same period, I had to attend a seminar in New Delhi. Accordingly, I took my new shoes which I valued so much and also kept a second older pair of shoes and packed them among other essential things and departed for my seminar. I wore the new shoes during my lecture on the first day. I was so charmed by the shoes that I kept them under my bed in the room where I was staying. Then the seminar ended and I returned. Next day, my wife enquired about the new shoes. After a few moments, I remembered that I had left the shoes under the bed and forgotten to take them on my return.

Akash, Lucknow

Answer: Instead of putting these shoes in the appropriate place, you kept them under the bed which is not normally done. Secondly, you were so anxious to go home that you did not check the room before you left.

This is a common experience that you forget to pack things when you leave your temporary stay in a hotel. It is advisable to make a checklist of all the places you need inside the room such as bathroom, drawers, wardrobe, bed, etc. Better to make use of few places as it will be easier to remember them.

Self Confidence

Q.5. I am a 65-year-old man working as a part time manager with an export house. In the last two years, I have been making a few mistakes which could have been avoided. Do I suffer from Alzheimer's disease or am I losing self confidence?

Bhupinder Singh, Chandigarh

Answer: Sometimes, occasional failures shake your confidence. This may happen due to memory loss. In such situations one often loses one's self reliability. The fact is that all of us, on some occasion or another, commit failures on trivial issues. It is simply not sensible enough to worry about. This is particularly true when we become older but that does not mean that persons are inflicted with a deadly disease like Alzheimer's. Of course, as we grow older our memory is not as good as it was.

So, no need to take this seriously. Such occasional memory lapses, as you mention, do not restrain you from socialism and neither do they create a health problem for you.

Umbrella Problem

Q.6. Vivek, Mohit and I had just moved into a flat in Ranchi. We had to present our research papers in HRD, HEC, Ranchi. As it was raining, I took my umbrella and went out for lunch with Mohit. Vivek had taken his raincoat. We took our lunch and discussed important issues. Meanwhile, it had stopped raining.

We went to present our research paper and then followed a serious discussion with other distinguished people who had come there. Now, the weather was good but after two days rains started again, then suddenly, I looked for my umbrella which I had forgotten to collect. After much search we were unable to find it.

Please make suitable explanation about my memory loss.

Gaurav, Ranchi

Answer: This is another case of missing the cues. Once the weather changed, you forgot about the umbrella. Had it been raining continuously, you might not have forgotten your umbrella. Vanishing of cue ('rain') was also supported by the lack of mutual social reminder. Mohit failed to even remind you.

Vanishing cues are serious causes of memory lapse, and it can happen to anyone. However, it is important to make a mental note of cues because once it has vanished little can be done.

House Keys

Q.7. Once we were invited to our friend's house, almost 40km away from our residence. We hired a car and on the way, we went for shopping. In the car, I had arguments with my friend on some trivial issues. After attending the party, we came back in the evening. We were also under the influence of alcohol. In our friend's house, we enjoyed ourselves very much. After a few hours, we decided to return. We did not stop to check who had the house keys before we left. We had also made usual checks before we left.

When we reached our home we were shocked to find that we had left the keys on the dining table of our friend's house. Now my friend, anyhow opened the main gate and was in search of a suitable brick to break into the room. To my surprise, I had left the back door unlocked. Thank God, nothing unfortunate happened.

Anonymous

Answer: As you were distracted by your own personal problems and arguments, you could not make proper checks before leaving. Secondly, under the influence of alcohol, you even forgot to take keys which you had left on the dining table.

This incident illustrates the multi-faceted nature of memory relapse. Over-indulgence and too much argument over trivial issues also played a part. Domestic arguments often disrupt social process and deviate your attention from even fundamental things. Moreover, being aware of those factors which distract can help you in future whenever you face such a situation.

Double Lunch

Q.8. Once we were invited to a dinner by my friends. On the scheduled day, my wife and I ate a full meal, unaware of the invitation. After a few moments my friends telephoned us and as a result we had to take a meal again.

Subhash, Agra

Answer: Lack of communication breaks the relationship. Surprisingly even your wife could not remind you, neither your friend talked to you. Such forgetfulness is a common incident. On the fixed date your friend should have talked with you. For such a reminder you can keep a calendar or personal date diary which will keep you abreast of your official and unofficial engagements.

Missing Laptop

Q.9. I am a software savvy executive and often visit places of business interest. Whenever I leave for an important assignment, I carry with me a palmtop computer to aid memory.

Once I had to present my views on computer and modern technology. The conference was organised in Mumbai. I booked my flight and reached the hotel room where I moved towards my destination. In the conference hall, I was in deep discussion with a systems analyst. After half an hour, I remembered that my palmtop was not with me. This electronic device is not only very useful but also costly. Anyhow I managed to get it later on.

Harjinder Singh, Ludhiana

Answer: This is yet another case of distraction caused by being involved in other activities. You forgot your palmtop because you were occupied with your engagement and conference. Failure to check properly also added to your woes.

Again, it highlights that every distraction appears due to negligence on the part of checking which is essential. Devices like palmtops should be kept in pocket after use.

Coat

Q.10. Sunil Bhatia invited me to lecture on Personality Improvement at JNU. Since it was a chilly morning, when I left I put on my coat. On arrival, I hung my coat on a hook in his office.

I lectured for a couple of hours and afterwards took some snacks and coffee. The weather had warmed up. After thanking

Bhatia for inviting me, I went to catch a train to return home. After I had travelled a few kilometres, I realized that I had forgotten to take my coat. Later on, Bhatia arranged to get my coat back.

Anu, Bangalore

Answer: This is a classic example of multi-casual memory failure. You forgot because you could not remember the cues.

Change in weather from cold to warm eliminated your need for coat. You were so engrossed with your conversation and lecture that you almost forgot every other thing.

This memory failure again refers to vanishing cues. This situation comes when the factor of reminding disappears from your memory. By putting your coat on hanger in the office, the cue vanished. Better to have made a mental reminder to ask for the coat before you left. Certain possessions like umbrella, coat, etc. are more likely to disappear from your memory sight.

Watering the Plants

Q.11. I love greenery around me and like plants but rarely remember to water them before they are dried—or worse. Why does this happen? Please suggest.

Kapil, Delhi

Answer: Although you love plants, you pay little attention to them as they are not in your priority. Loving and caring are two different aspects. As the intervals between are long and vary from plants to plants, it makes it difficult to remember them. This type of forgetfulness is insidious. By the time the reminder cue surfaces, it is too late. Sometimes lack of motivation to care for them also is a causal factor. There are many people who are devoted to their plants and also manage them successfully.

Forgetting the Suitcase

Q.12. Sujata and I had booked a weekend break to Shimla, some eight hours' drive from my residence. Sujata as usual had packed all the needful things in a suitcase. We along our children departed on our journey. When we were half-way, I asked her if she had put the suitcase in the car. To my shock, she replied in the negative. Again we had to drive back and restart our journey. Why do such careless situations occur?

Anuj Panday, Delhi

Answer: Communication between you and your wife may have broken down for sometime. You were too much dependent upon your wife and thought that she would have surely carried the suitcase. Neither you reminded her during the packing about things to be done. Had you put the suitcase in the proper place, you might have noticed it when you started for the journey. It is yet another case of missing physical cues that led to memory failure. You should also have exchanged conversation that might have paved the right way.

Things on the Car Roof

Q.13. It has become almost a habit that whenever I drive to work I take a cup of coffee with me. My mug has a wide flat bottom and it can easily be kept on the dashboard. Usually, I put the mug on top of the car when I open the backdoor.

One day, I put my cup on top of the car and then found out that my wife had just parked her car nearby. After throwing my car in first and second gear I searched my coffee mug when I found that it was not on the dashboard. A little later I found the cup was still on top of the car. A little annoyed I looked both sides to see if any passersby had noticed it.

Subhash, Bombay

Answer: This is also a case of distraction. May be your wife's sudden appearance with her car near you worked as a distracting agent. So, instead of blaming your wife, make her happy so that in future you will avoid annoying yourself. Lack of proper checking of items you carry often disturbs concentration.

Office Building

Q.14. On several occasions, when I was new to the job, I found it difficult to leaving the escalator of my office building and turning left when I should have turned right and vice versa. Of course, I was correct most of the time but such error in judgement put me in an embarrassing situation. However, there are other people who often make similar mistakes. I tried my best to recollect the exact position but failed to do so because the foyer on every floor was exactly same.

Anonymous

Answer: Like other people, you too failed to remember whether you had taken the east or west elevator. In such a situation, the only solution is to realise its insidious nature and pay more attention to which elevator you are taking. Of course, this is not a common problem.

But, then, a few have the knack of committing errors even if they are not supposed to do so.

Finding the Photographs

Q.15. Before going abroad for an important assignment, I had to send a set of photographs/drawings of historical figures to a publisher who was to publish my first book. For two days, I picked up the photos and prepared an envelope so that I could send it to him. But when I decided to send them, I could not find them anywhere.

As expected, I panicked and after searching for hours, I went to the photographer and begged him to provide new sets. When I returned from abroad I found the photos in a folder. I was shocked at the loss of my memory.

Anonymous

Answer: You forgot where you put the photographs because you made the mistake of not keeping them in a 'safe' place. It is common practice that a valuable should be kept in a safe place.

You need to get benefit from a well-organized filing system or storing items in convenient places you can easily remember.

Road Map

Q.16. During my academic days, I used to attend regular class at a premier institute. The institute follows a haphazard design, due to which I often forgot the way from the entrance to the classroom. Please help me.

Ragini, Mathura

Answer: This often happens when driving a car on a road which is familiar but where you have to turn off at some junction which is not unusual for you. Some people have great difficulty in learning the routes, even if they regularly pass through them. They rarely take trouble to learn the map of the route. It is yet a common experience when, someone fails to remember even familiar directions, routes and buildings. This is probably because most people assume that they will remember and consequently do not make the effort to work out the layout of a route or building. Often, forgetting a route is not a great problem because you can easily ask the way. On occasions, it can be serious when you end up in a bad or disturbed area.

One should be aware of the problem and make a conscious effort such as remembering landmarks, map and writing down directions.

Locking the Car

Q.17. Locking the car is a common practice by car owners. One day, I put the key in my overcoat pocket instead of my trousers pocket. After some time I decided it was too warm to wear the overcoat, so I unlocked the car and threw my coat into the back seat and shut the car door. I arrived at the place after my work and I looked for my keys and realized that the keys were inside the car.

Lokesh, Agra

Answer: Such a thing is one of the most common instances of memory failure. Although it is a regular practice, this time you put your keys in your overcoat pocket.

An additional or spare car key is needed to avoid such a situation. A little bit of distraction stops your attention from checking where actually you put your items. So always make a habit of putting keys in your pocket or purse.

Water Tap

Q. 18. One day, when I was working in Mumbai, the water supply was turned off at 7 a.m. (when I was taking bath). After my bath, I left for the day. On my return I saw my flat flooded with water.

Himani, Srinagar

Answer: This is a good example of missing the reminder, physical cues. Had the water been running, you would have turned off the taps.

This is one of those things which need no real solution. Never leave the bath taps running in case you feel distracted. Similarly if you have finished cooking turn off the burners. Almost everyone has had such experiences. It is not an exact case of memory failure.

However, make a habit of being alert while leaving your flat and also double check important things like taps, burners, windows, lights, etc.

Signing the Credit Card

Q.19. These days, I suffer from a certain kind of forgetting which is embarrassing and annoying. I use my credit cards on several occasions. I hand the credit cards and talk to the assistant waiting for my card status. Some stores give their own receipt and also need the credit card slip to be signed by the card holder. On some occasion after receiving the store receipt I attempt to walk out without signing the slip unless the storekeeper says, "You have to sign your credit card slip". Depending on how one looks at the event it may appear that I am trying to get away without paying the bill. My behaviour looks suspicious although I do not have any intention to do so.

Sunil, Bangalore

Answer: There may be two important reasons for the failure. While buying things your mental activity makes you forget the credit card transaction. Secondly, because different stores follow different methods for credit card holders, you may forget signing the slip.

It would be helpful if all stores used the same system. Then everyone would get into the same routine. Now you may use a visualization method to overcome this problem. Close your eyes and see the whole event, visualize yourself signing the slip and taking the card back. Try to do this exercise 5 to 10 times (it will take around a minute for a single exercise). Now by doing so you have highlighted your memory problem and next time whenever you are in a shop, this exercise will come as an automatic reminder.

Appointment

Q. 20. For more than two decades, I have been taking tutorial classes for students and job-seekers. As far as I can remember, I never failed to turn up to such tutorials. Last year the system was changed to make it more efficient. Tutorial times were rearranged by the administrator. Surprisingly, this year, I failed to turn up on at least three occasions.

Madhu, Calcutta

Answer: The change in environmental set-up leads to memory failure. Change in time created an atmosphere of confusion and even a regular fellow like you missed on some occasions.

Remembering something also depends on how you arrange your daily routine. Using a diary, though not a foolproof mechanism, can solve this problem provided you regularly consult your diary. Reverting to the older system may again resolve the problem.

Speech

Q.21. Three years ago, I together with my colleague, Ramanuj, agreed to present a lecture, to the Psychology department, Patna University. All went smoothly until the very last line when I went completely blank as I could not remember the whole point of the paper. I had come here without any notes. Even my colleague could not help me as he was quite busy in other activities.

Upma, Kanpur

Answer: Over-confidence and failure to come with complete preparedness led you to such a messy affair. However, this problem is one of the easiest to solve. Whenever you give a special speech, no matter how prepared you are, always keep short notes of the main points in your pocket or purse. Too much dependence upon your memory system, ironically, leads you to decapitation and such embarrassment.

Birthday

Q.22. I have just started my academic career in a Central university, far away from home. Just four days back I happened to be in my home and as usual decided to see my best friend Vineet who was putting on an expensive coat. I commented on this to him. To my utter surprise, he replied that he was given this as a birthday present. At this point, I realized that I could not remember his birthday although he was very close to me.

Bhupinder, Moga

Answer: Forgetting birthdays, anniversaries, etc. of a friend or loved one is a common but a major problem. It is also an indication that you do not care as much for your near and dear. Of course, it will be helpful if your friend starts giving hints about important days and discusses presents on such occasions. Few people deliberately avoid mentioning birthdays or anniversaries and expect their friends to know in advance. The best way is to keep a record in your diary and always refer at the beginning of each month to see whether it has some important day or not. Also try to memorise important dates using Phonetics method.

Names/Faces

Q.23. One day, a woman, working in another part of the office and a little bit known to me, met me and we exchanged words. I thought I had met her earlier and she was Sangeeta, although I noticed her resemblance with yet another women named Neha. After some time while returning from Mumbai, I encountered her again and called her 'Sangeeta'. When I was just few steps past her, I realised that she was Neha. I felt embarrassed and apologized for my mistake.

Jaswant, Pune

Answer: Calling people by wrong names is out of etiquette, partly arising from comparing two people who look similar. Over-confidence is another significant factor in this case and occurs regularly with those who are less efficient in checking and have a history of memory failure.

If you are not sure about the person's name, identify and confirm before calling him/her. Also use the technique given in this book to learn names and faces.

Christmas Card

Q.24. As a true professional and a Christian, I make it important to exchange Christmas cards with my secretaries. One year Bessy joined as a secretary and I forgot to give her a card. In a hurry, I got out to get the card, forgetting to remove my spectacles, without which I cannot read. I signed the card and presented it to her.

She read the card and then handed it to other secretaries who, after seeing the card, started laughing. Because I had forgotten my spectacles, I could not realize that the card was obscene and an inappropriate Christmas gift. It put me in embarrassment.

Mini, Goa

Answer: It has been observed that Christmas time is peak for memory failure. And such a mishap can happen to anyone. Because of your initial embarrassment at having forgotten to give a card, you rushed to rectify the situation and forgot to ensure that you had spectacles with you.

There is no real solution to his kind of problem. How could one know that forgetting one's spectacles would lead to the selection of an obscene card on a religious occasion like Christmas? It has nothing to do with memory failure.

Waiting for a Friend

Q.25. I and a host of friends arranged to go out to a bar on a Saturday night and at the last moment, one of them came and said that he was going out to get food and requested us to wait for a few minutes. After a few moments we all rushed towards the bar forgetting that we had left that fellow behind us, who later on made sarcastic notes to me.

Krisnu, Surat

Answer: This is the result of "out of sight out of mind" syndrome. As your friend disappeared to get food, he was not there to remind you of his presence.

It is useless to expect your friends to wait for you if you go off when others are about to set out to enjoy themselves. This is certainly not a case of memory failure, so no need to worry when we are engaged with several people in a jovial mood, we often forget one who left between the time. In such a situation even as a host you forget to remind others about someone. Social integration demands energy and a wider perspective.

Briefcase

Q.26. I and my friend Manoj went for lunch at a restaurant near Osmania University. After lunch, we discussed various aspects of business for the Sociology Department and for University. We returned to the office at the university. Later, after 2 hours I received a call from the owner of the restaurant telling me that I had left my briefcase and that I could pick it up at my convenience.

After one year, we again lunched there and as usual discussed important issues. I sat down and put my briefcase by my side. We paid and left. As we were a few steps ahead, the owner of the restaurant came running out and shouted that I had left my briefcase.

Anonymous

Answer: Due to your engagement which required socialising and indepth discussion, you could not put significance to your briefcase. Had you carried a bigger item, it would have been harder to forget.

It is yet another common phenomenon forgetting an item like a briefcase which may not be carrying important documents is often reported from individuals who are related to academic activities. Keeping the briefcase in your line of vision is one way of solving this problem. (Also read the chapter on absent-mindedness in the book).

Historical Dates

Q. 27. I am an Arts graduate and preparing for IAS examination and opted for History as one of the subjects. My biggest problem is memorising historical dates. I always confuse between the dates. I revise the dates several times periodically by writing and also by reciting them. Nothing helps. I would be thankful to you if you suggest to me some methods for committing them perfectly to memory.

Aman, Banaras

Answer: The only and foolproof way of learning anything is through association and visualization as I have already suggested in the book. The things learnt just by rote learning without association or with very weak association are lost easily. Let us take some examples to understand how to learn the dates perfectly.

1. 1921: Gandhiji assumed leadership of Congress Party.
2. 1933: Hitler became Chancellor of Germany.
3. 1922: Mussolini marched to Rome.
4. 1927: T.V. demonstrated for the first time.

Exercise I: (1921) Gandhiji assumed leadership of Congress Party.

Close your eyes and visualize Gandhiji addressing a party meeting as a leader. Now associate the mental picture with 21. We can link it easily if we think that Gandhiji is standing on 2 and holding 1 with his one hand. The sketch below will give you a little idea on how to visualize it.

Exercise II: (1933) Hitler became Chancellor of Germany.

Visualize a clear picture of Hitler. For Germany we can further visualize that Hitler is surrounded by **Many Germs**. Here we have broken Germany phonetically so that we may have perfect picture for Germany. Now connect the visualized picture with the shape of 33. Imagine the shape of 33 as a big moustache being replaced by Hitler's original small one.

Exercise III: (1922) Mussolini marched to Rome.

For 22 we can easily visualize two ducks (see sketch below). Now connect those ducks with Mussolini. For Mussolini we can think of MUSLIMS (phonetic conversion). Visualize two Burkha (for MUSLIMS) wearing ducks marching.

Exercise IV: (1927) T.V. demonstrated for the first time.

Visualize a television. Try to see it as clearly as possible. Now imagine you are connecting the television wire to a lamp-post. Refer to the sketch given below for clarity.

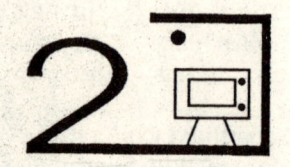

MOST USEFUL DIAMOND DICTIONARY

FEATURES

- A classic, abridged, handy and user-friendly dictionary of standard English to English words.
- Easy-to-grasp definitions written in an explicable vocabulary of 20,000 words.
- Words refer to derivatives where necessary. Abbreviations offer quick meaningful pursuits. These are used briefly to keep the dictionary concise.
- Diphthongs have been briefly explained to offer the words with correct angles of pronunciation.
- All words for day-to-day use have been chosen with a view to limiting it as a pocket dictionary. **Rs. 170/-**

FEATURES

- Extremely useful for translation because it gives not only the practical derivative but the root-word and synonym for the entry.
- Transitive and intransitive verbs have been given separately.
- Each word has been taken as a separate entry.
- All the technical terms used in Modern Sciences, Arts & Humanities, Industry, Banking, commerce, Administration etc. have been given.
- Each shade of the meanings of words, with a variety of meanings have been given.
- Compiled with special emphasis on authenticity & unambiguity.
- An up-to-date dictionary with extensive coverage of the prevalent words. **Rs. 170/-**

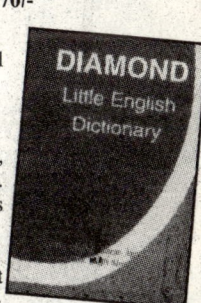

- आधुनिक ज्ञान-विज्ञान, चिकित्साशास्त्र, विधि, न्याय, अधिकोषण, शासन, कला-वाणिज्य आदि की पारिभाषिक शब्दावली से युक्त हिंदी का महत्वपूर्ण शब्दकोश
- प्रत्येक शब्द एक स्वतंत्र इकाई के रूप में प्रयुक्त
- बहुअर्थी शब्दों की प्रायः सभी अर्थ-छायाओं को देने का प्रयास
- मुहावरों और लोकोक्तियों का अर्थसहित संकलन
- क्रियाओं के अकर्मक व सकर्मक रूपों की स्पष्ट प्रस्तुति
- सामान्य कोशों से सर्वथा भिन्न आपका विश्वसनीय साथी

मूल्य : 150.00

- हिन्दी से अँग्रेजी अनुवाद के लिए सर्वथा उपयुक्त
- अँग्रेजी अर्थ मूल शब्द के पर्याय रूप में उपलब्ध
- क्रिया के सकर्मक व अकर्मक दोनों रूप विभाजित
- बहुअर्थी शब्दों की सभी अर्थ-छायाओं को देने का प्रयास
- आधुनिक ज्ञान-विज्ञान, प्रौद्योगिकी, चिकित्सा, कला, वाणिज्य, विधि-न्याय, अधिकोषण, शासन एवं सामान्य व्यवहार में प्रयुक्त शब्दावली का समुचित समावेश
- प्रामाणिकता का विशेष ध्यान   मूल्य : 150.00

Order books by V.P.P. Postage Rs. 20/- per book extra. Postage free on order of three or more books, Send Rs. 20/- in advance.

DIAMOND POCKET BOOKS (P) LTD.
X-30, Okhla Industrial Area, Phase-II, New Delhi-110020,
Phones : 51611861- 65, Fax : (0091) -011 -51611866, 26386124

OUR BEST SELLERS

IMPOSSIBLE...POSSIBLE
Biswaroop Roy Chowdhury

This book is about change. People by nature are status quoists. It is a state of mind. But those who are able to change, they succeed faster than those who remain tied to their old habits, mindsets and prejudices. This book will tell you how you can change the way you think, act and behave. It requires a little effort. But the results will be phenomenal. The chronic patients can recover, the habitual failures can turn around and the die-hard pessimists can become incorrigible optimists.

THE SECRET OF HAPPINESS
Jas Mand

Happiness is a state of mind of a human being, which is manifest in a consistent attitude of contentment. There are numerous examples in our daily life which illustrate that individuals with similar outside conditions have different frames of mind and hence varying degrees of happiness. It is not something that exists outside you.

SECRETS OF SUCCESS
Kapil Kakar

Thoughts originate from mind and by implementing those thoughts we get a result. In this book you will find in length about mind not only scientifically but also what Lord Krishna said about it. The topics covered in this book are the basics of life. If you don't have sound basics then you cannot move ahead in life no matter how much you pray. This book is for people of all age group as it can help students not only to develop their personality but also handle academic stress in a better way.

Come On! Get Set Go
Swati-Shailesh Lodha

This book is a genuine 'mirror' for you to introspect and evaluate yourself. It is not the run-of-the-mill stuff dealing with success and personality development. It focusses on "Failure" and its various facets. Read what a failure is, does and thinks and then refrain from it. Your friend, guide and philosopher is here to motivate you and make you not "The Best" but "Second to None".

For Trade Enquiries & Catalouge contact
Publisher and Exporters of Indian Books, published more than 1000 titles.

ⓞ FUSION BOOKS

X-30, Okhla Industrial Area, Phase-II, New Delhi-110020, Phone : 011-51611861, Fax : 011-51611866
E-mail : manish@diamondpublication.com, Website : www.diamondpublication.com